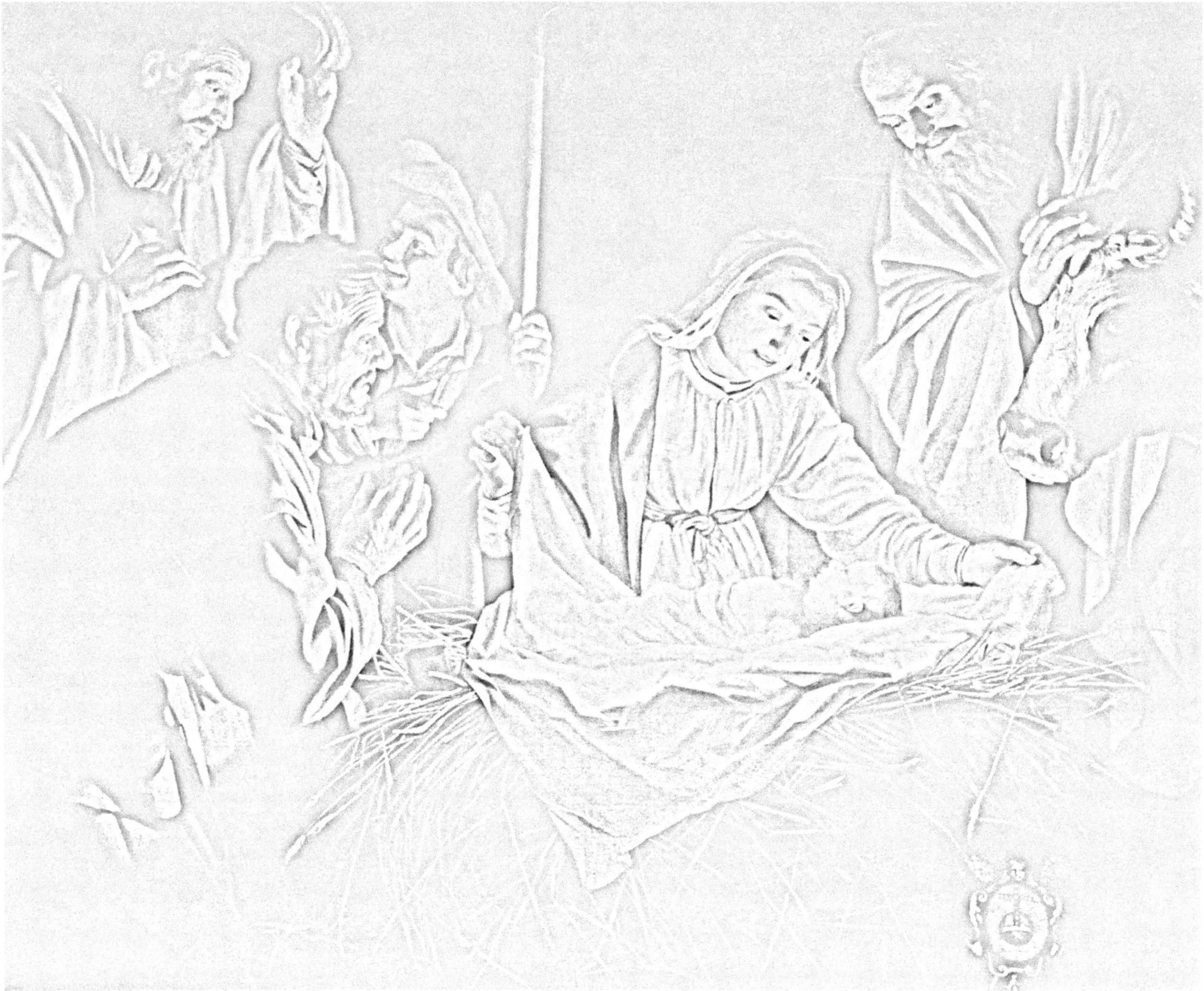

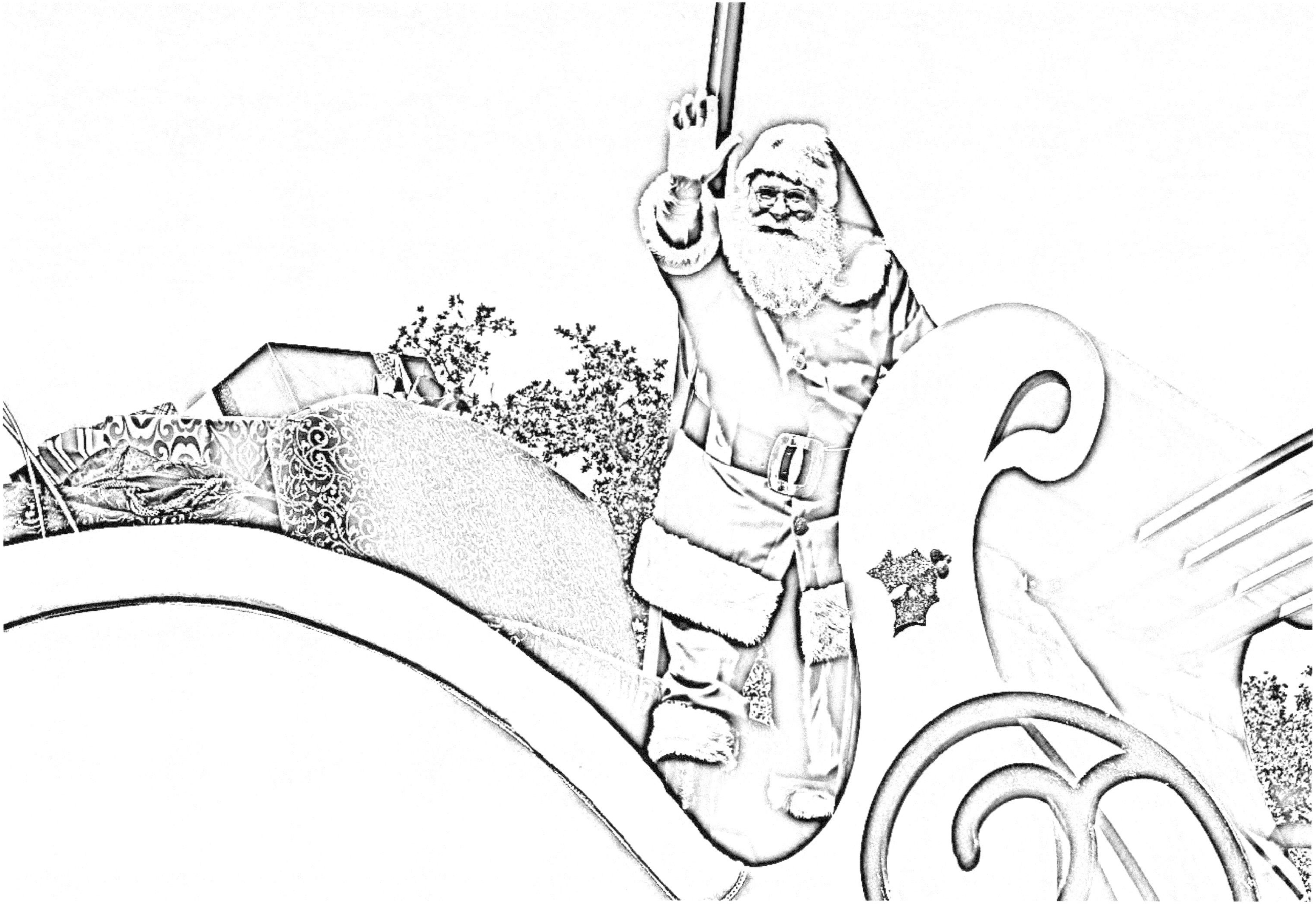

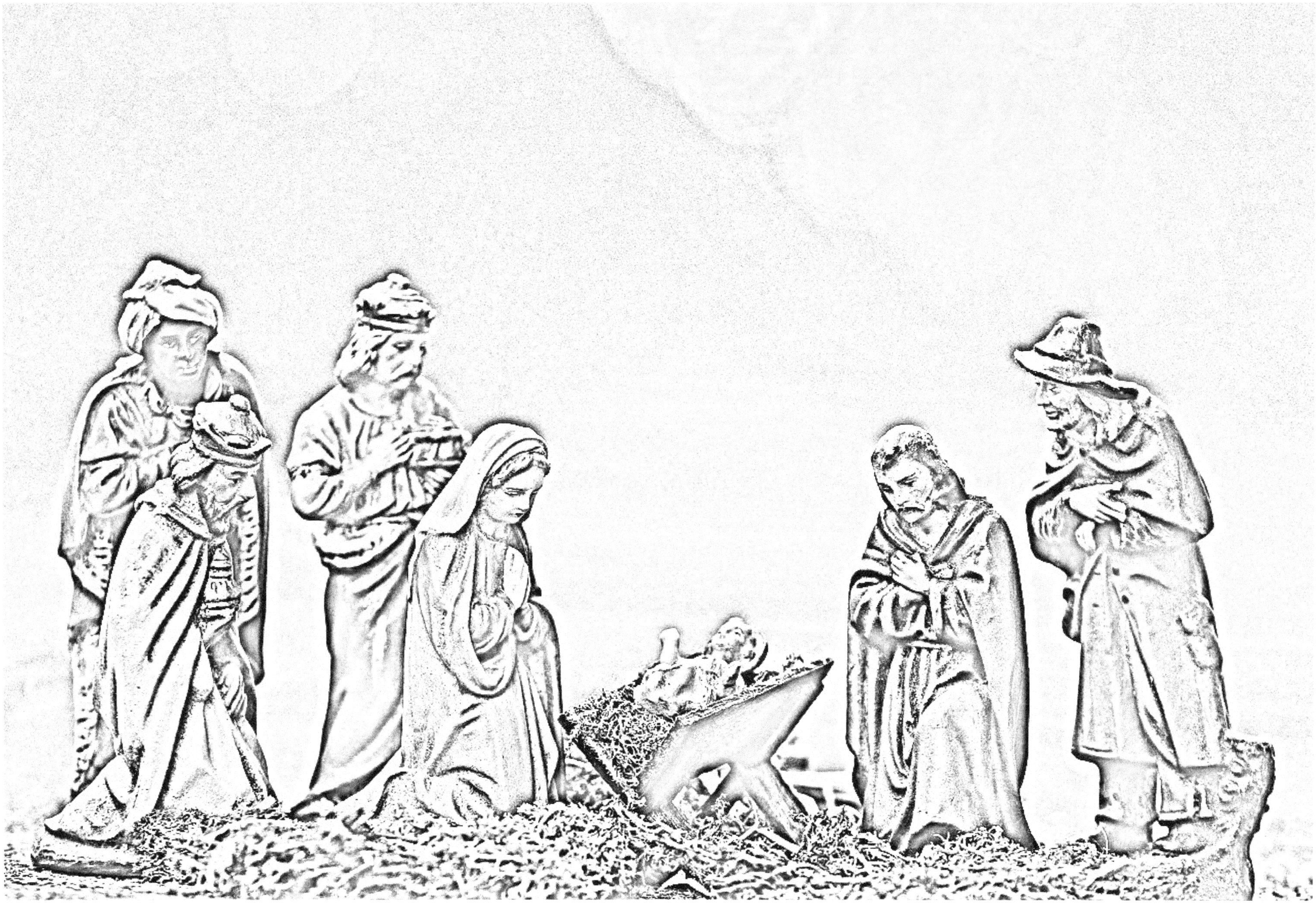

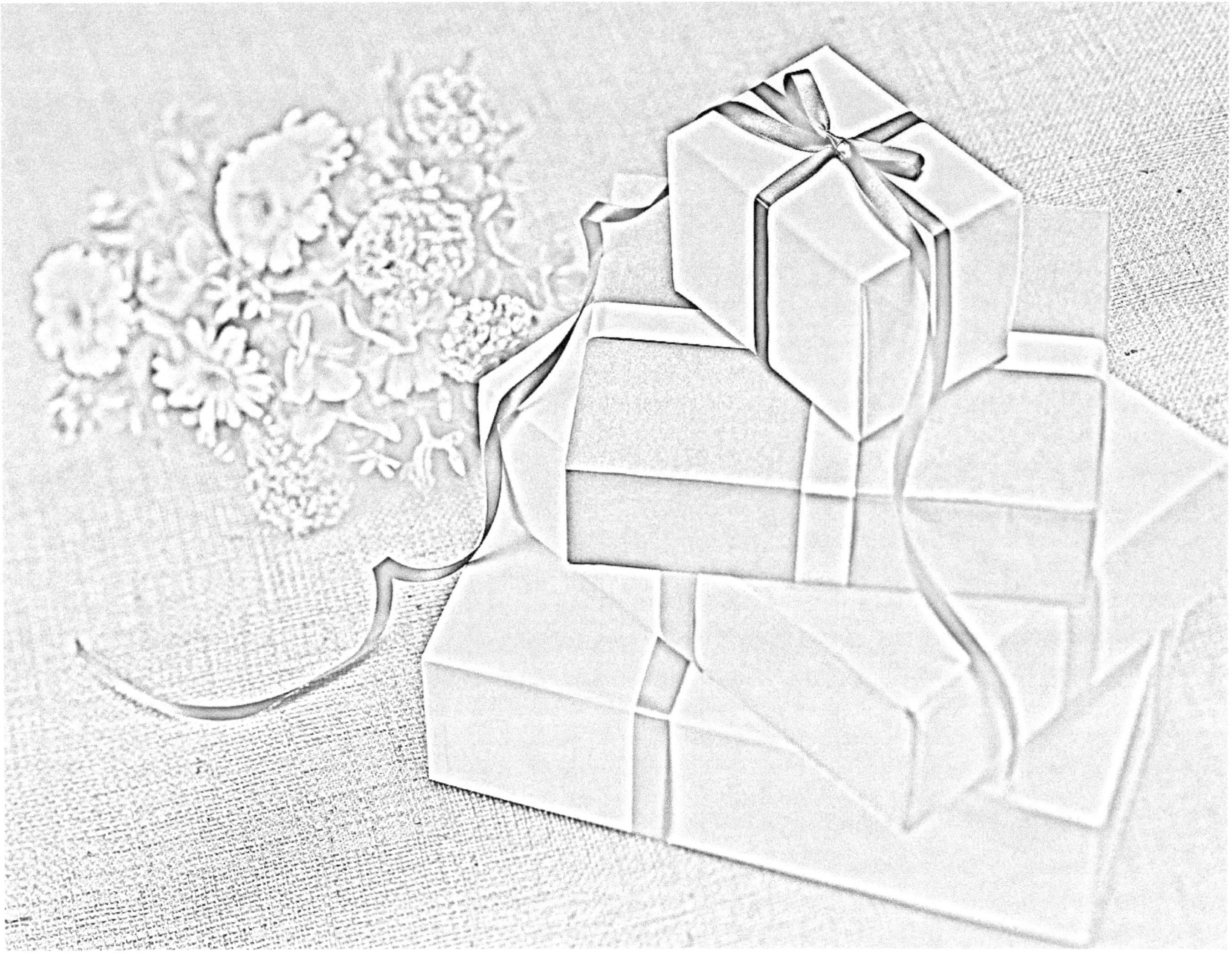

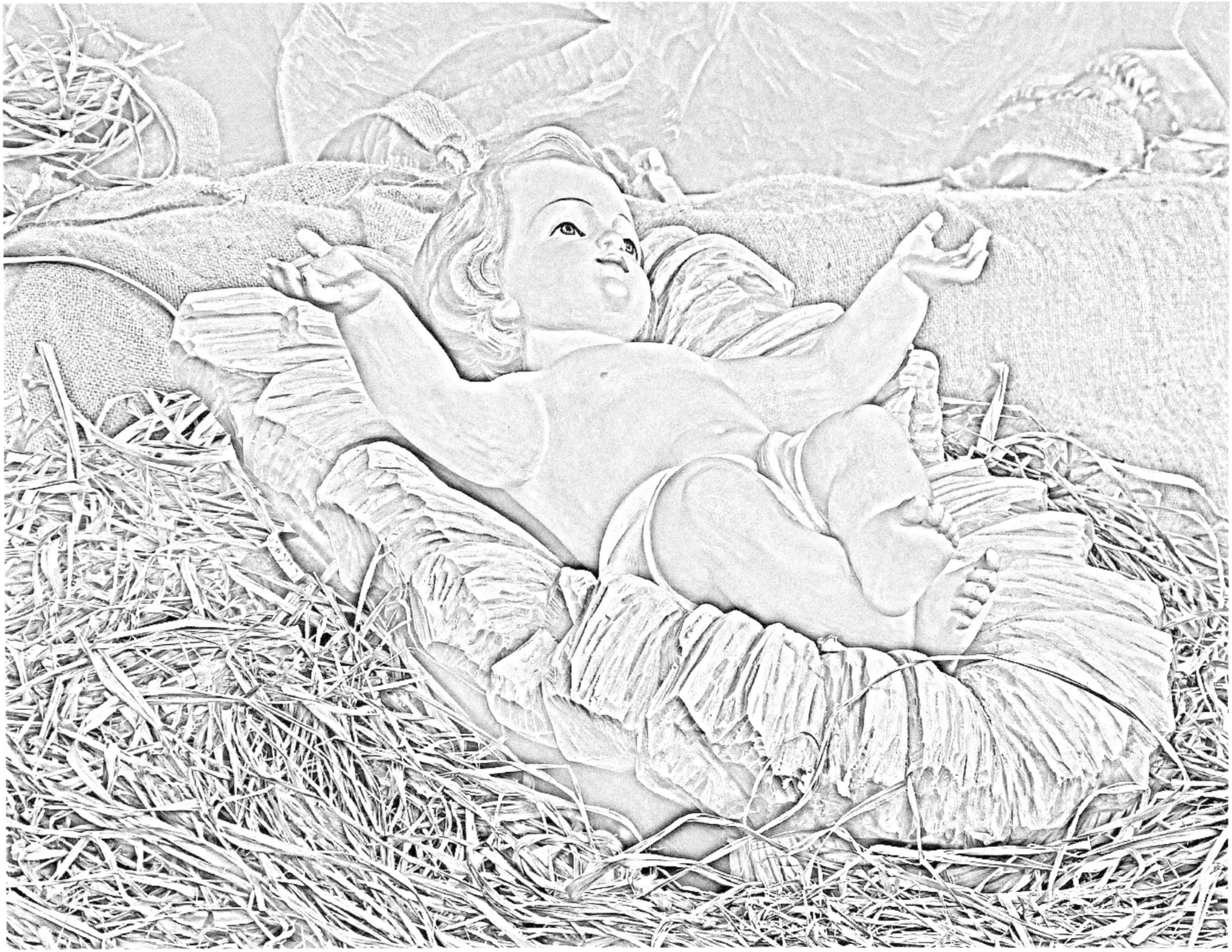

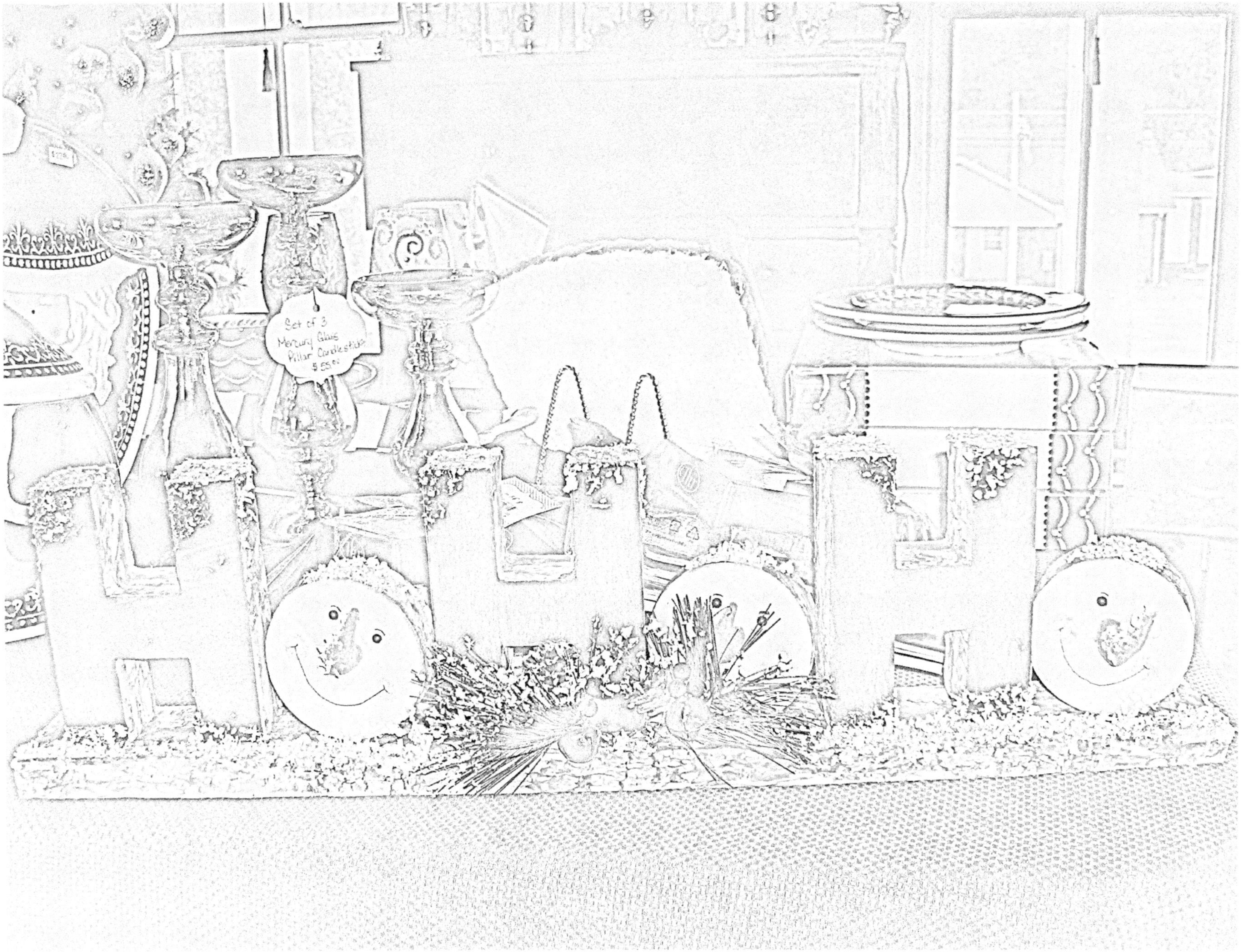
Set of 3
Mercury Glass
Pillar Candlesticks
$55.00

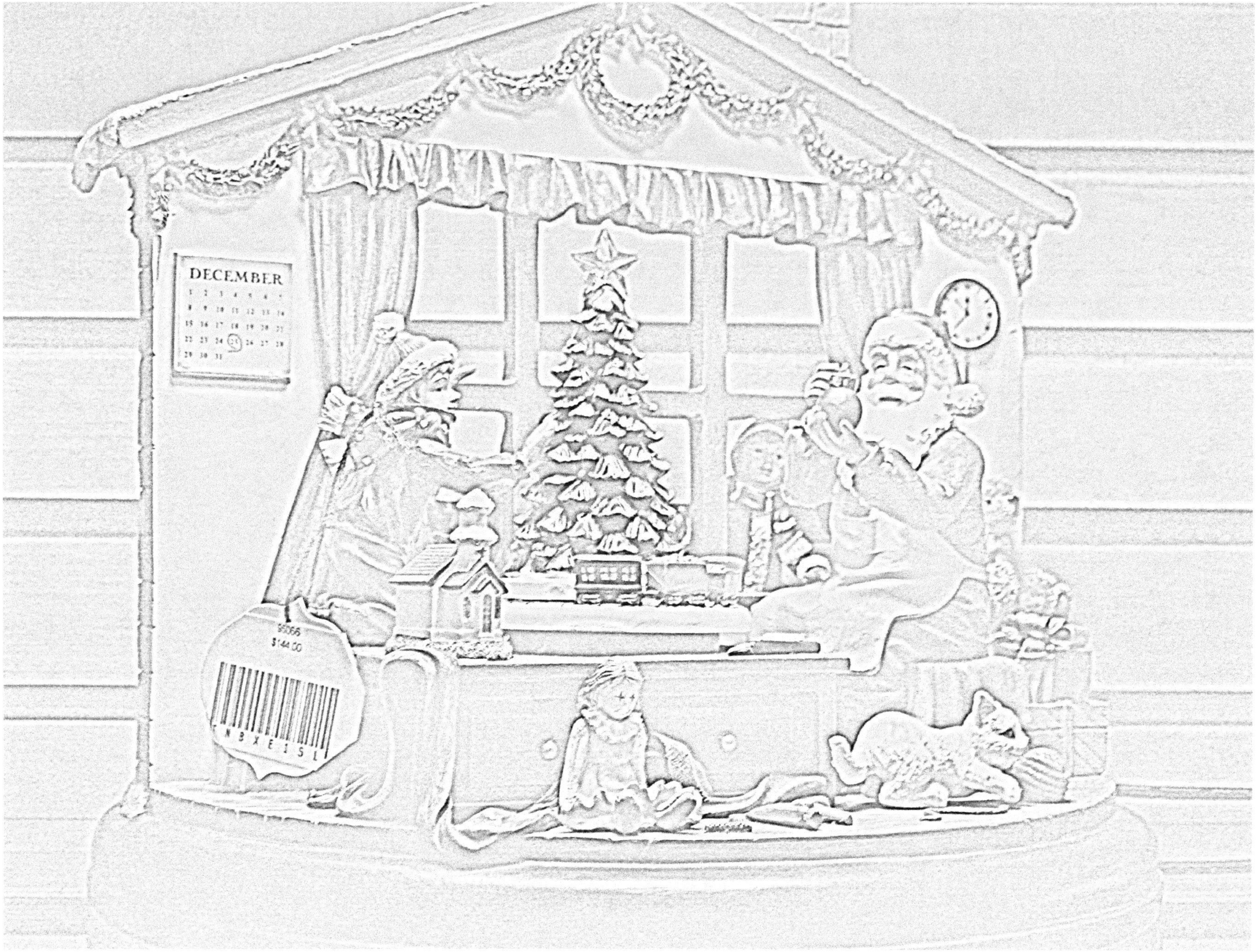
DECEMBER
95066
$144.00

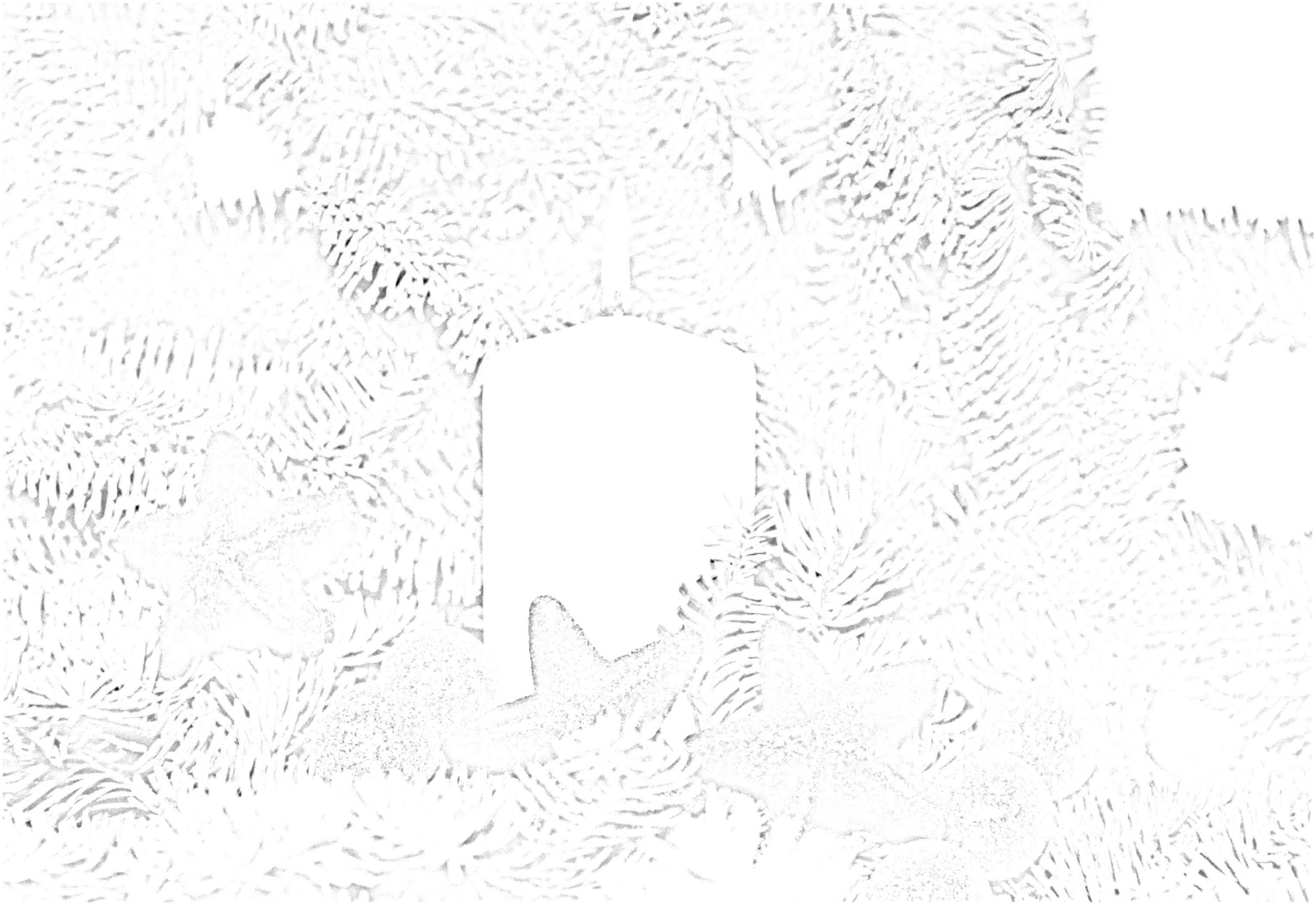

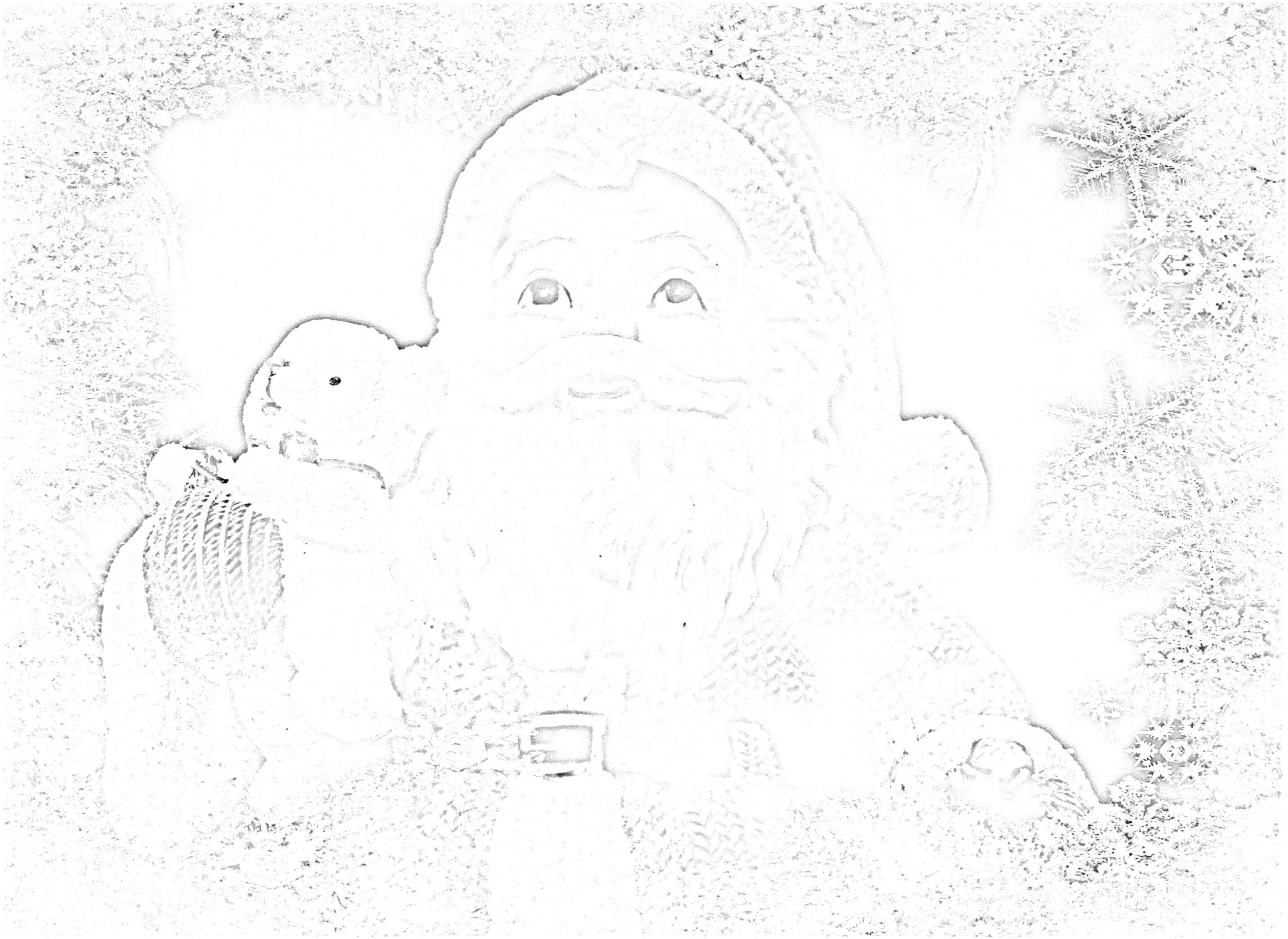

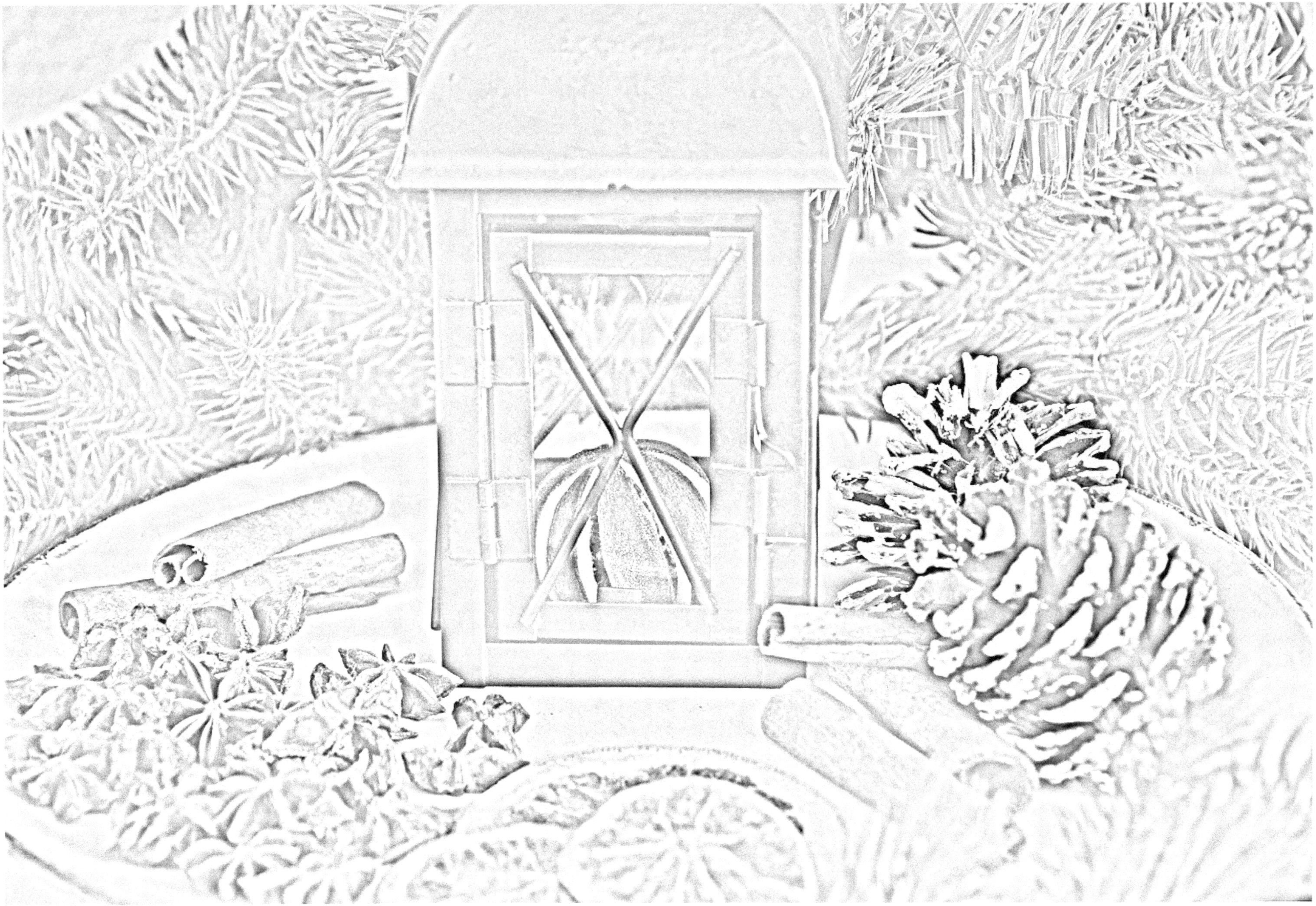

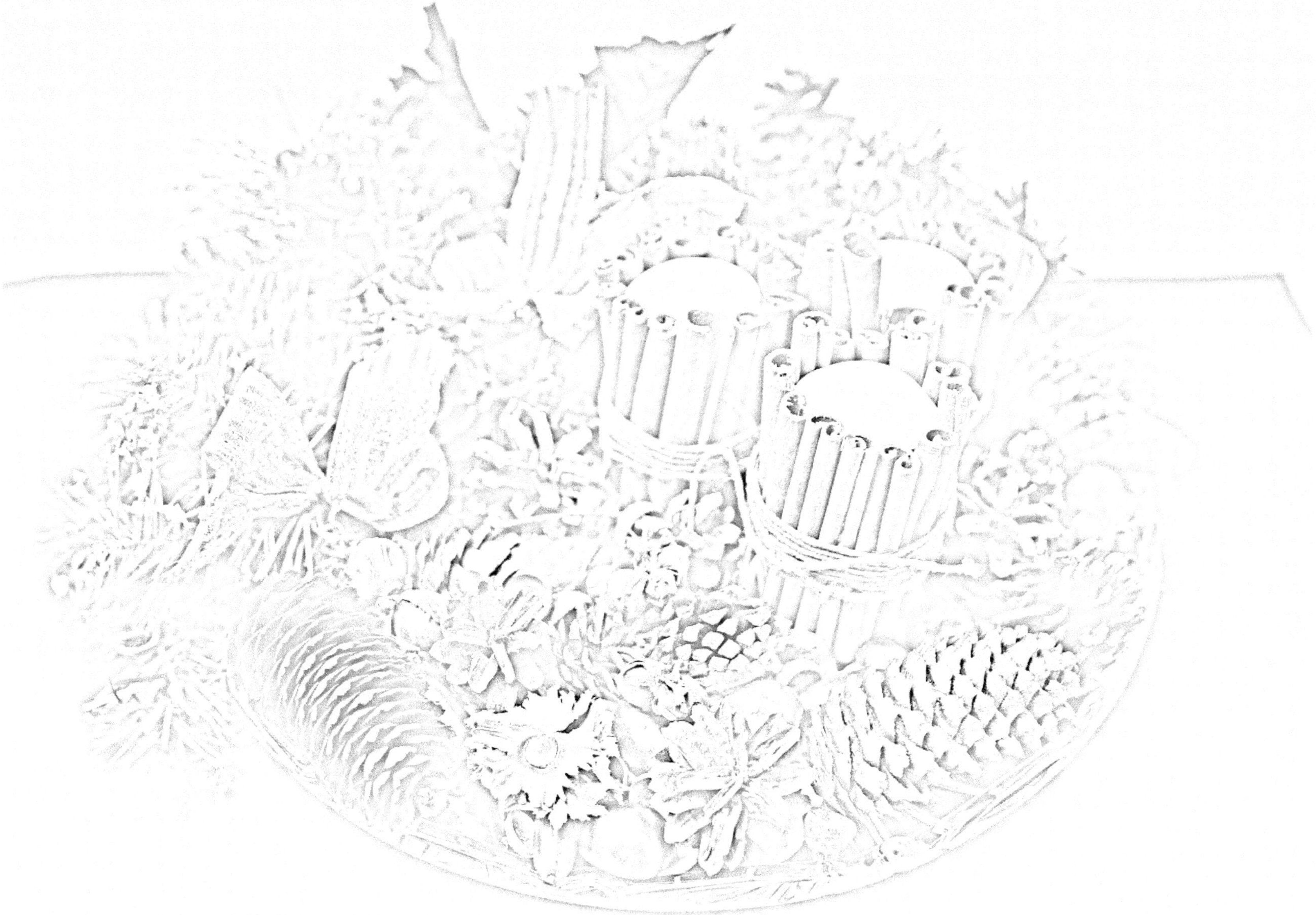

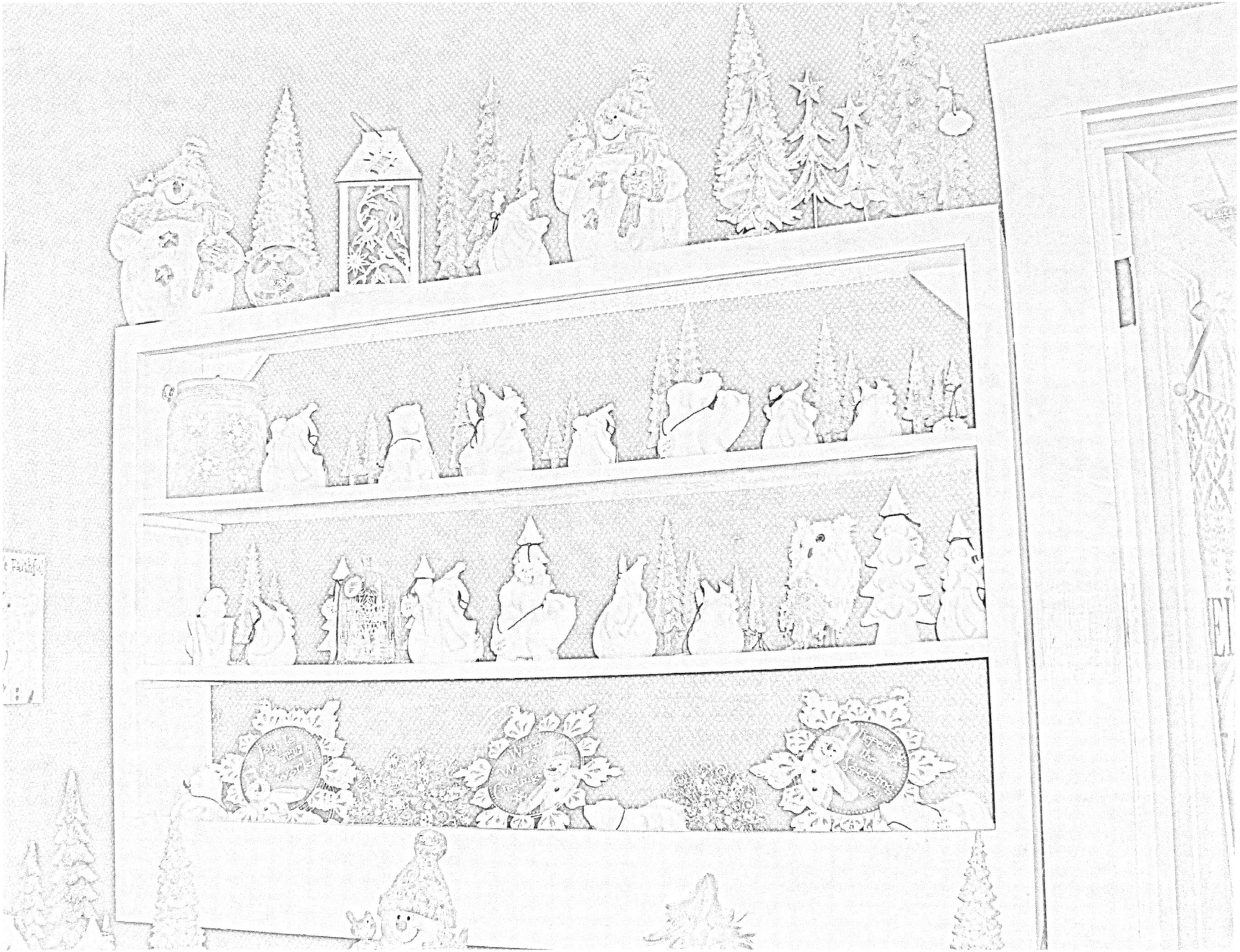

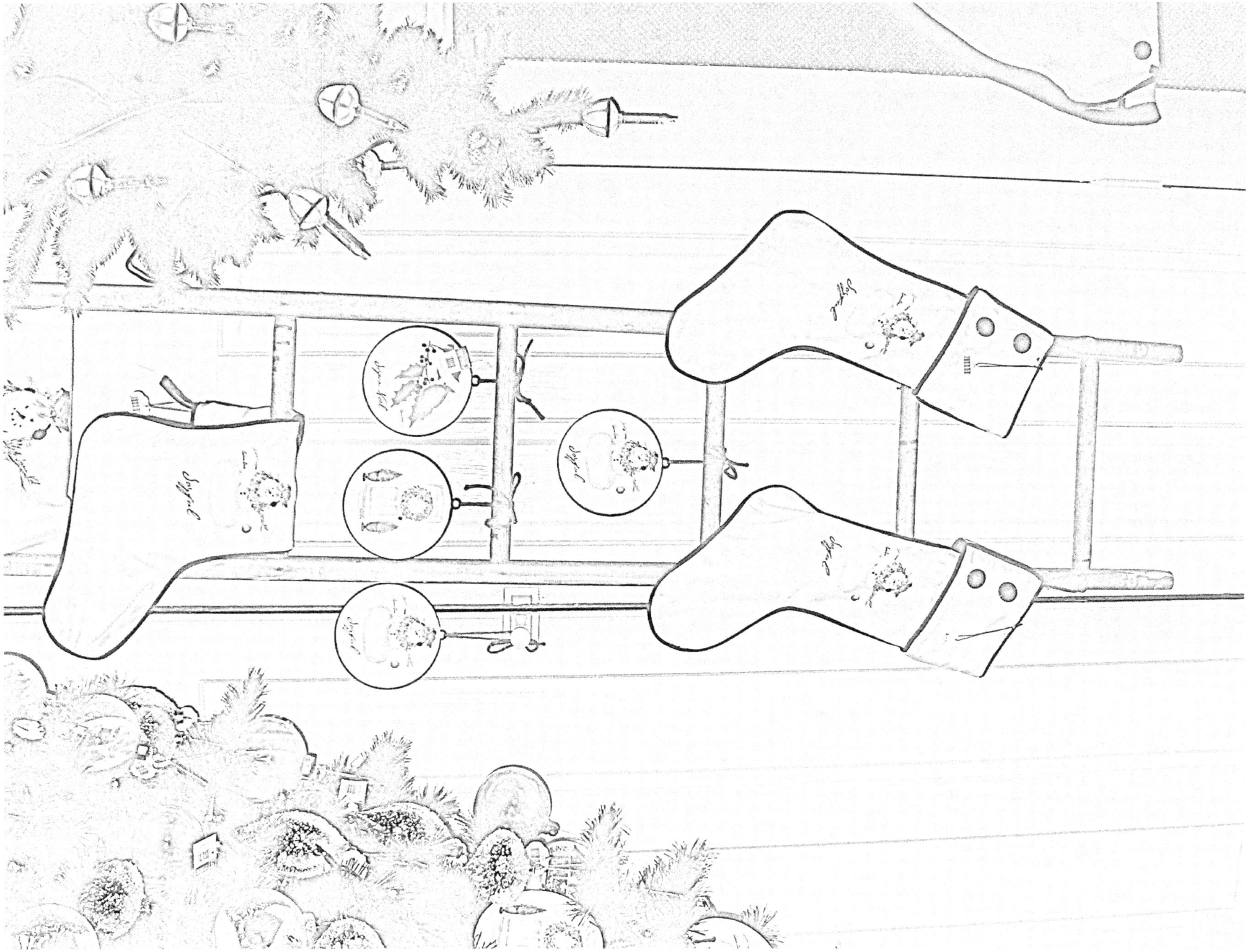

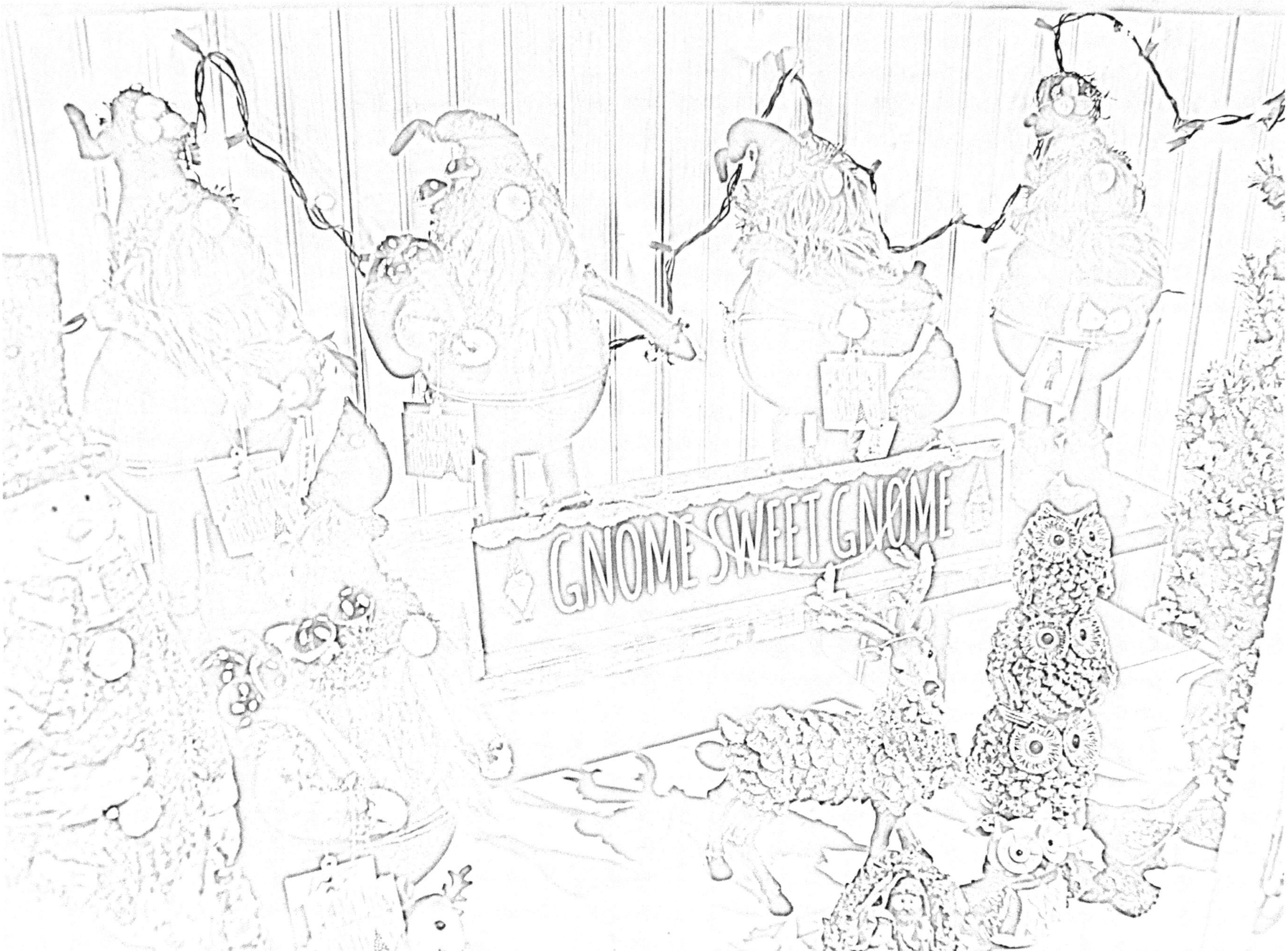
GNOME SWEET GNOME

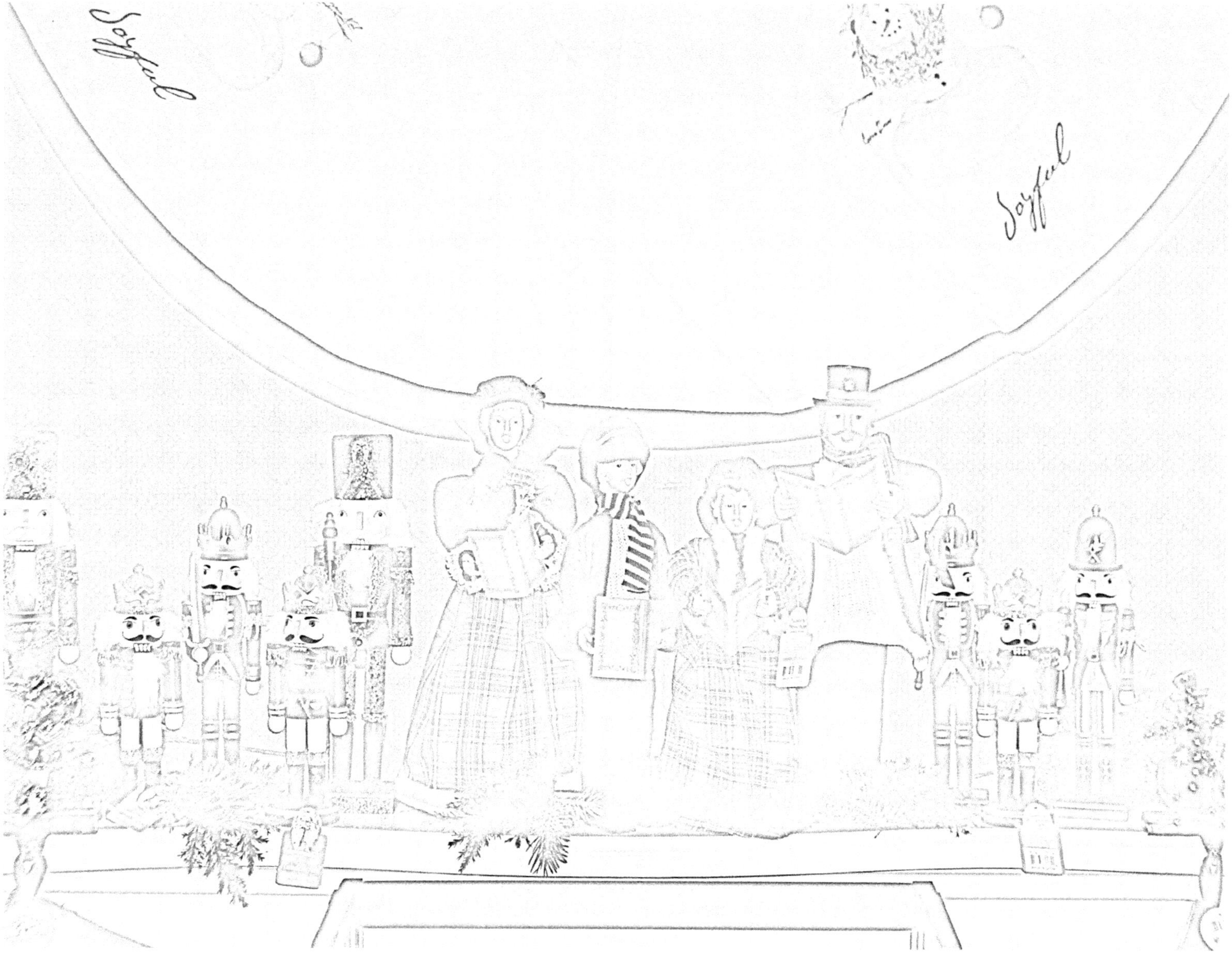
Joyful
Joyful

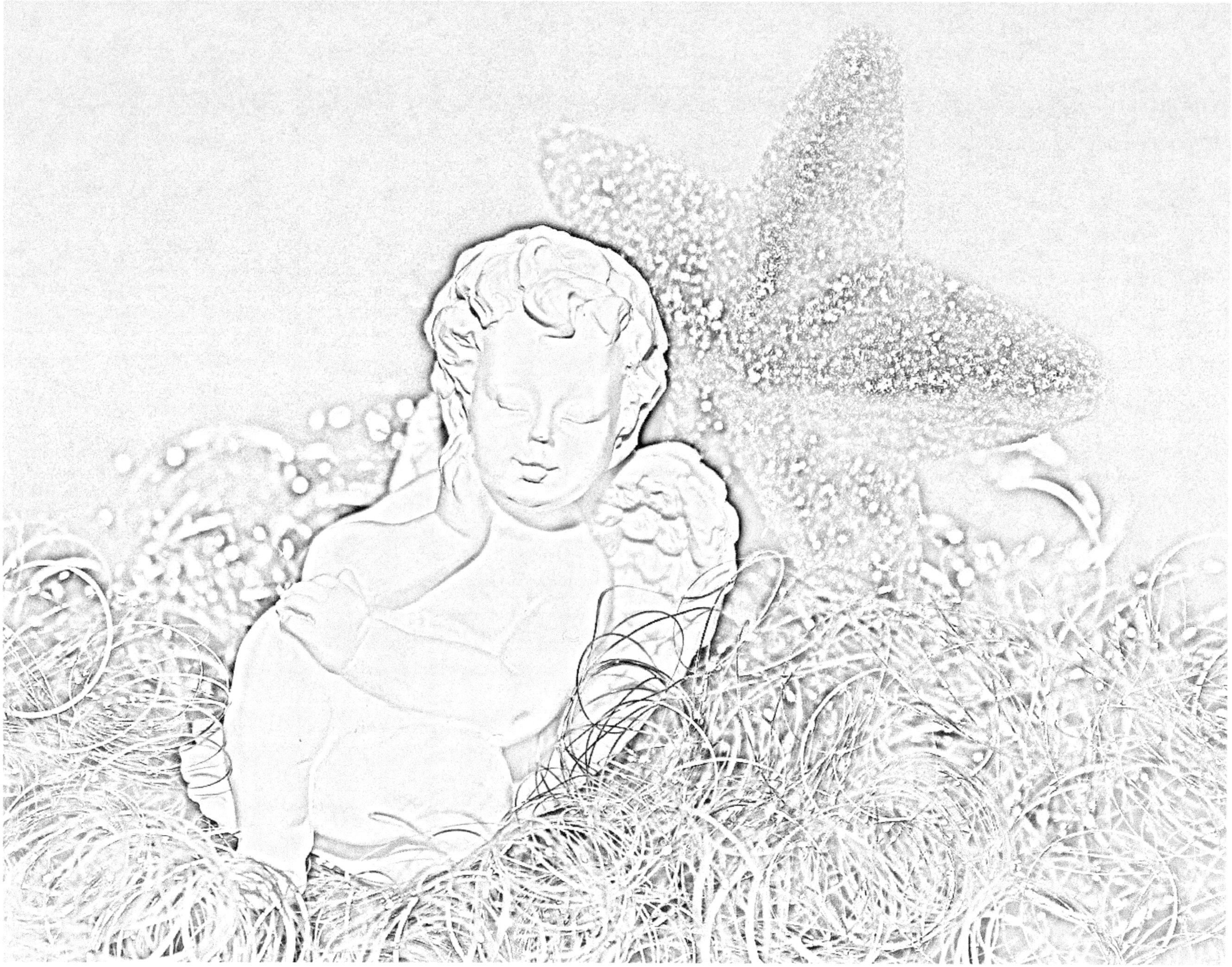

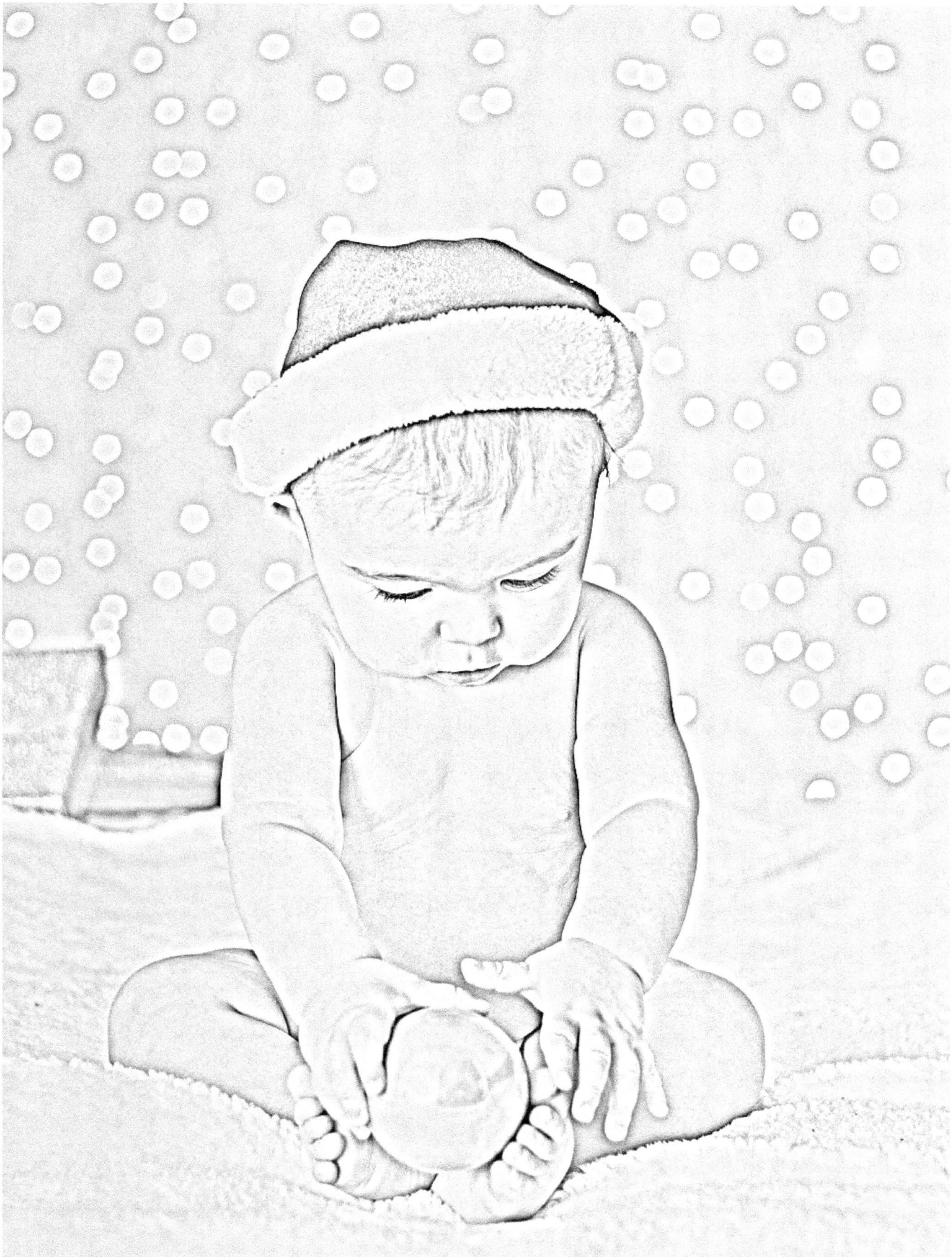

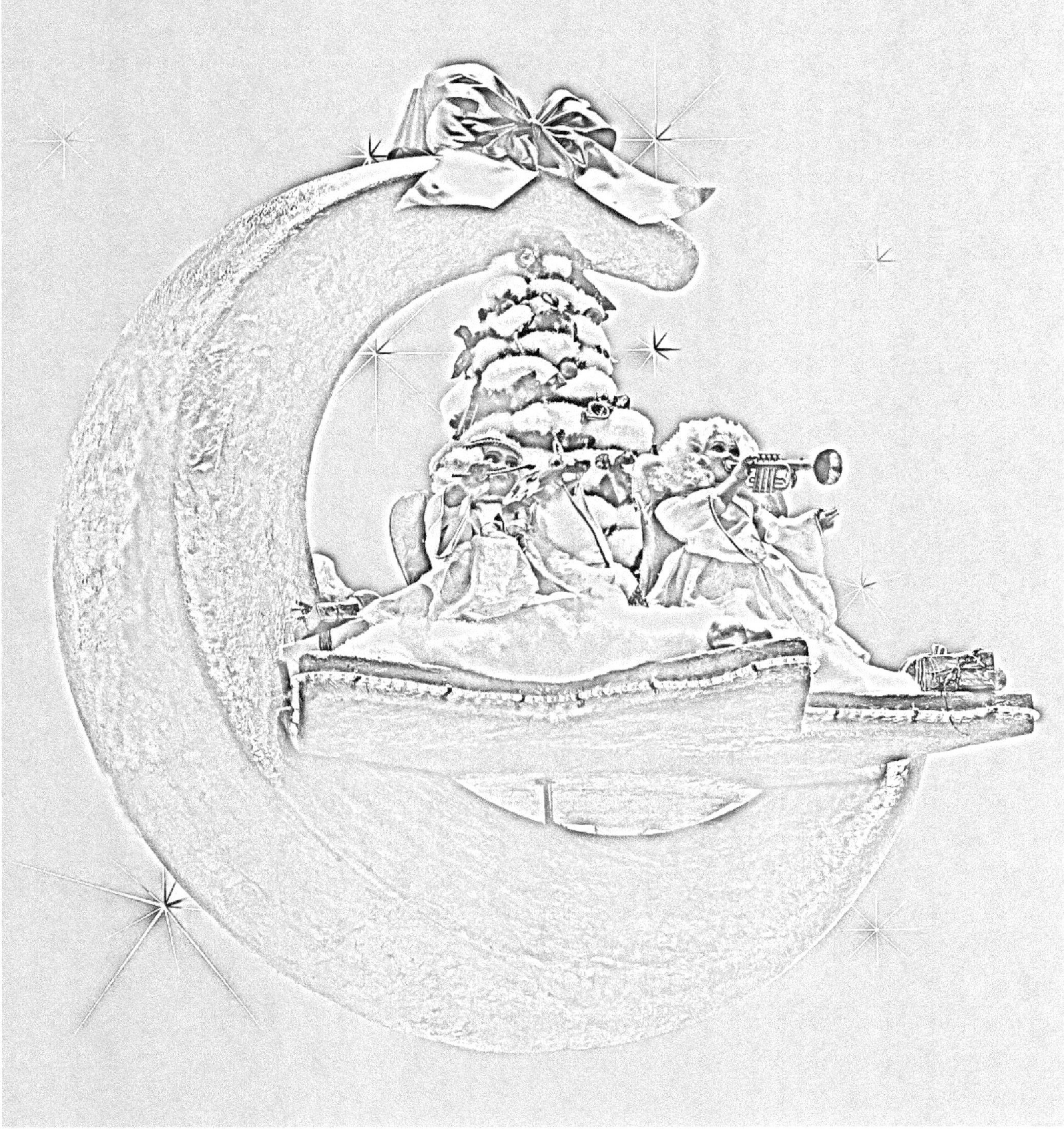

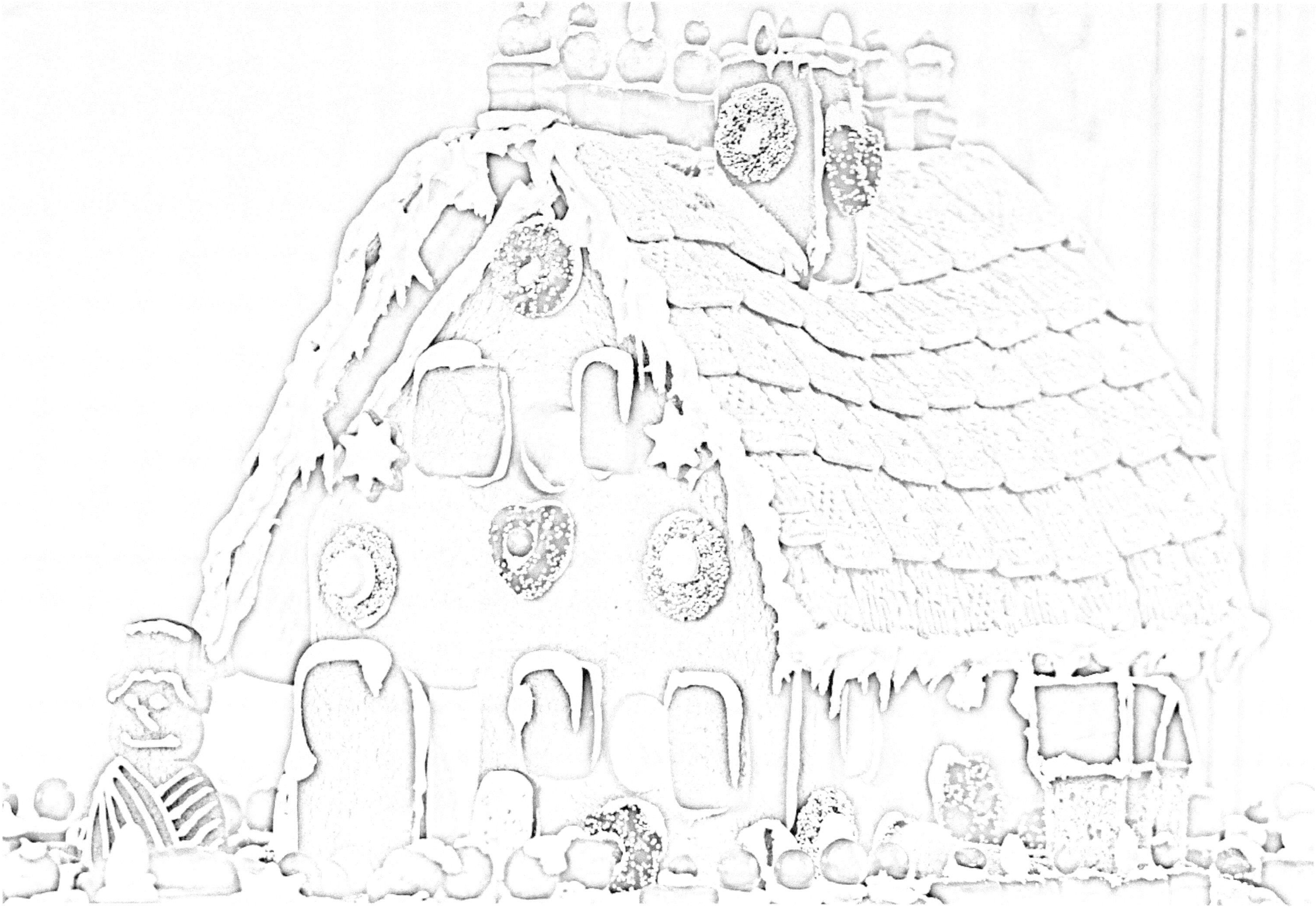

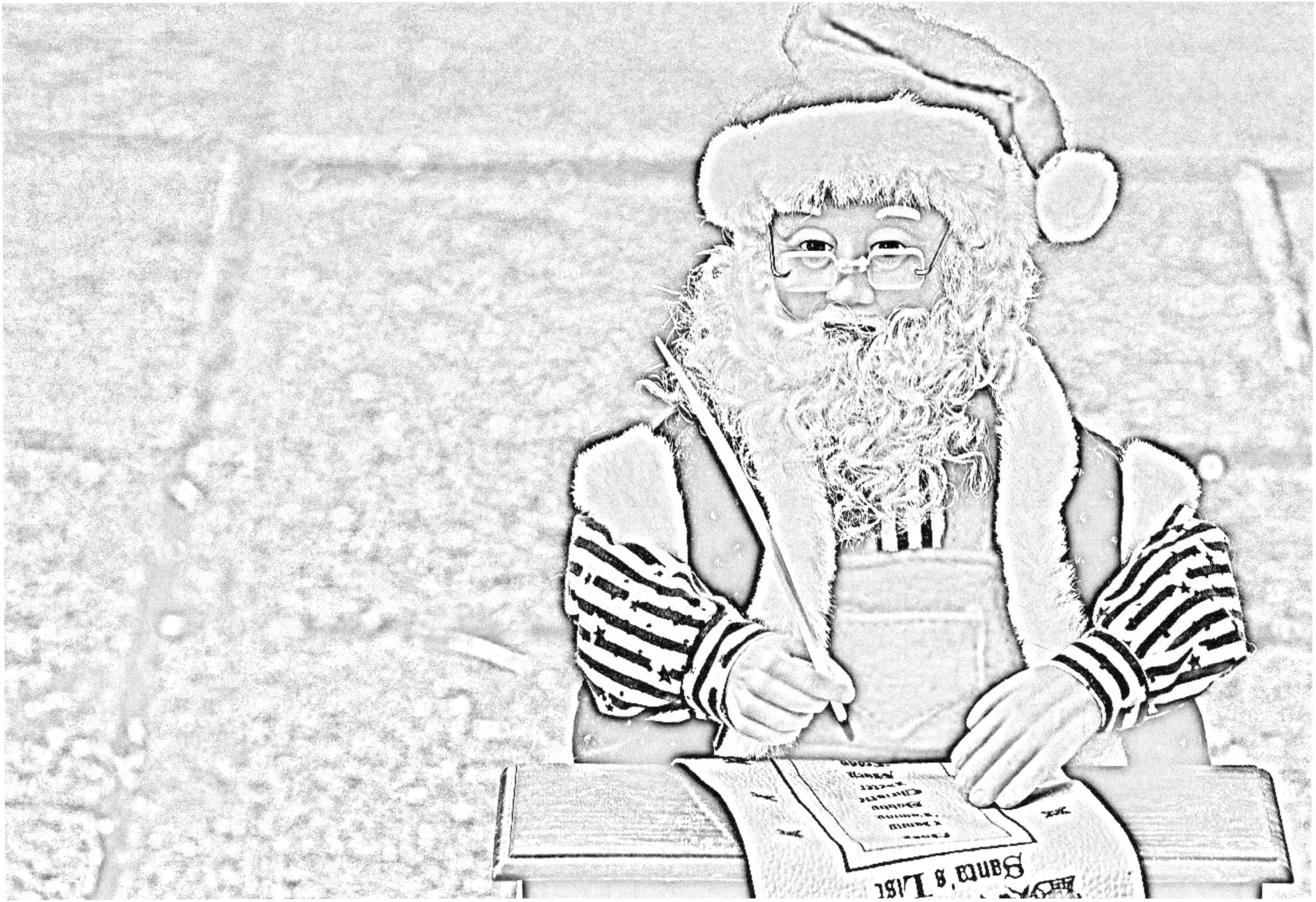
Santa's List

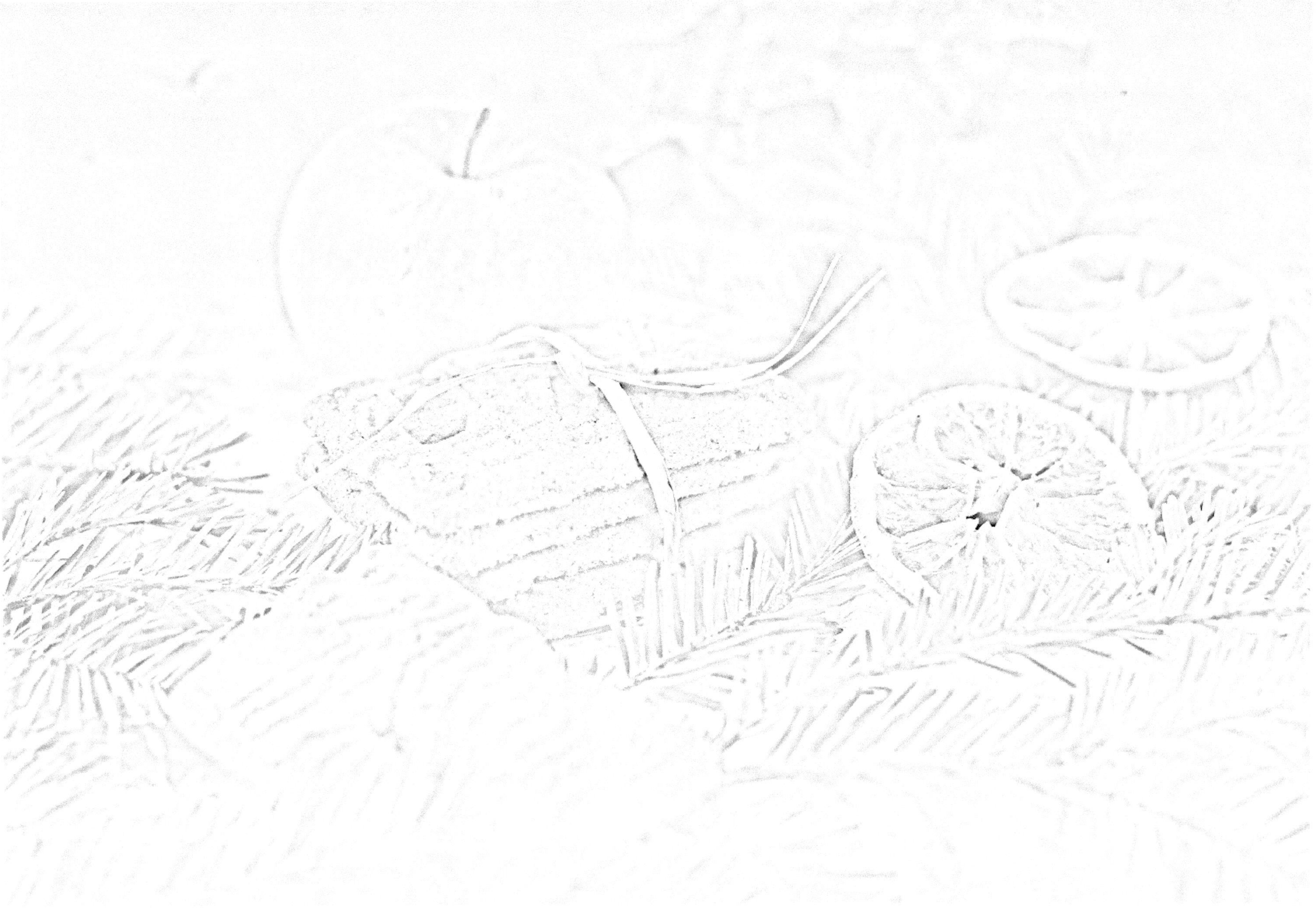

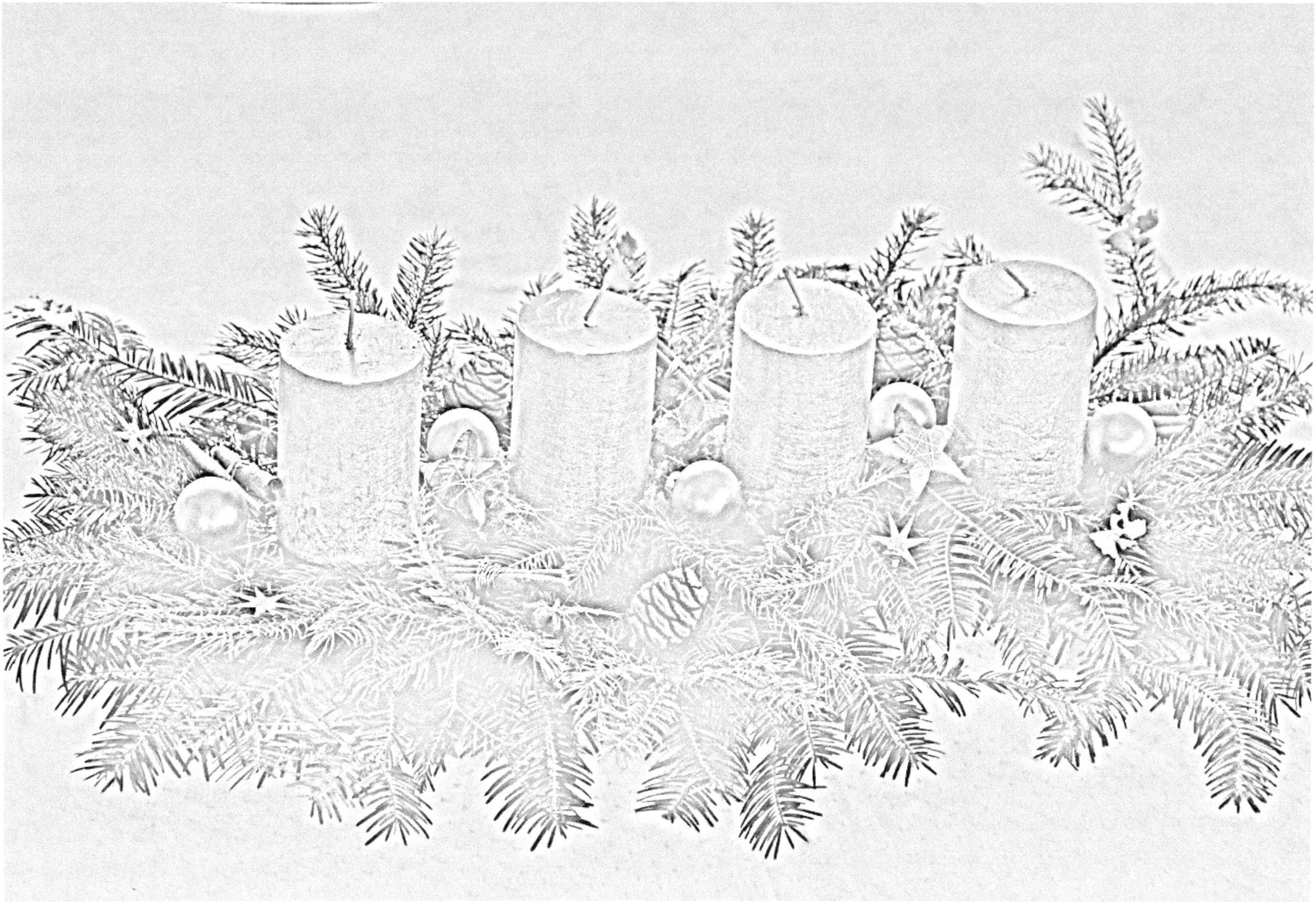

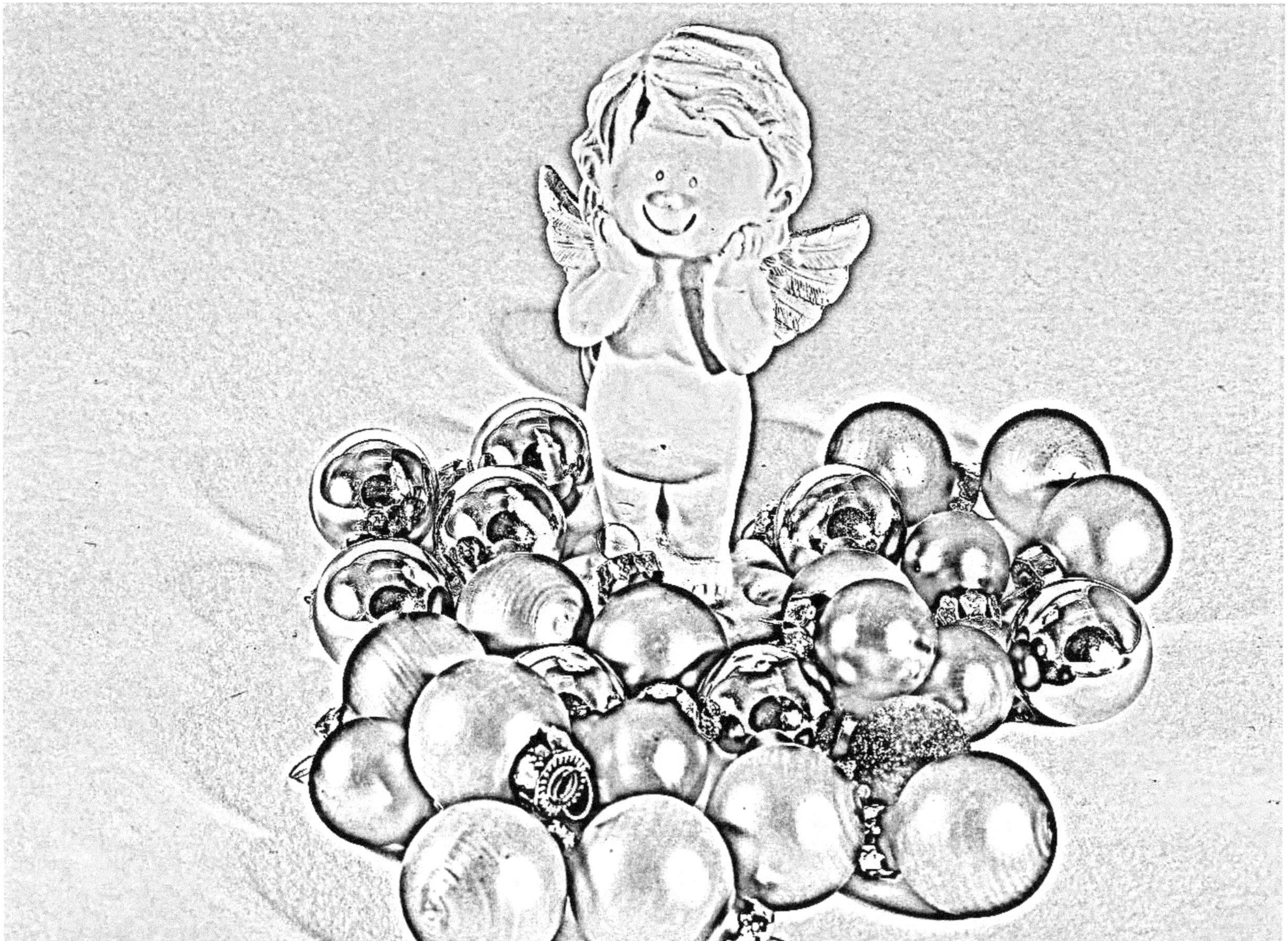

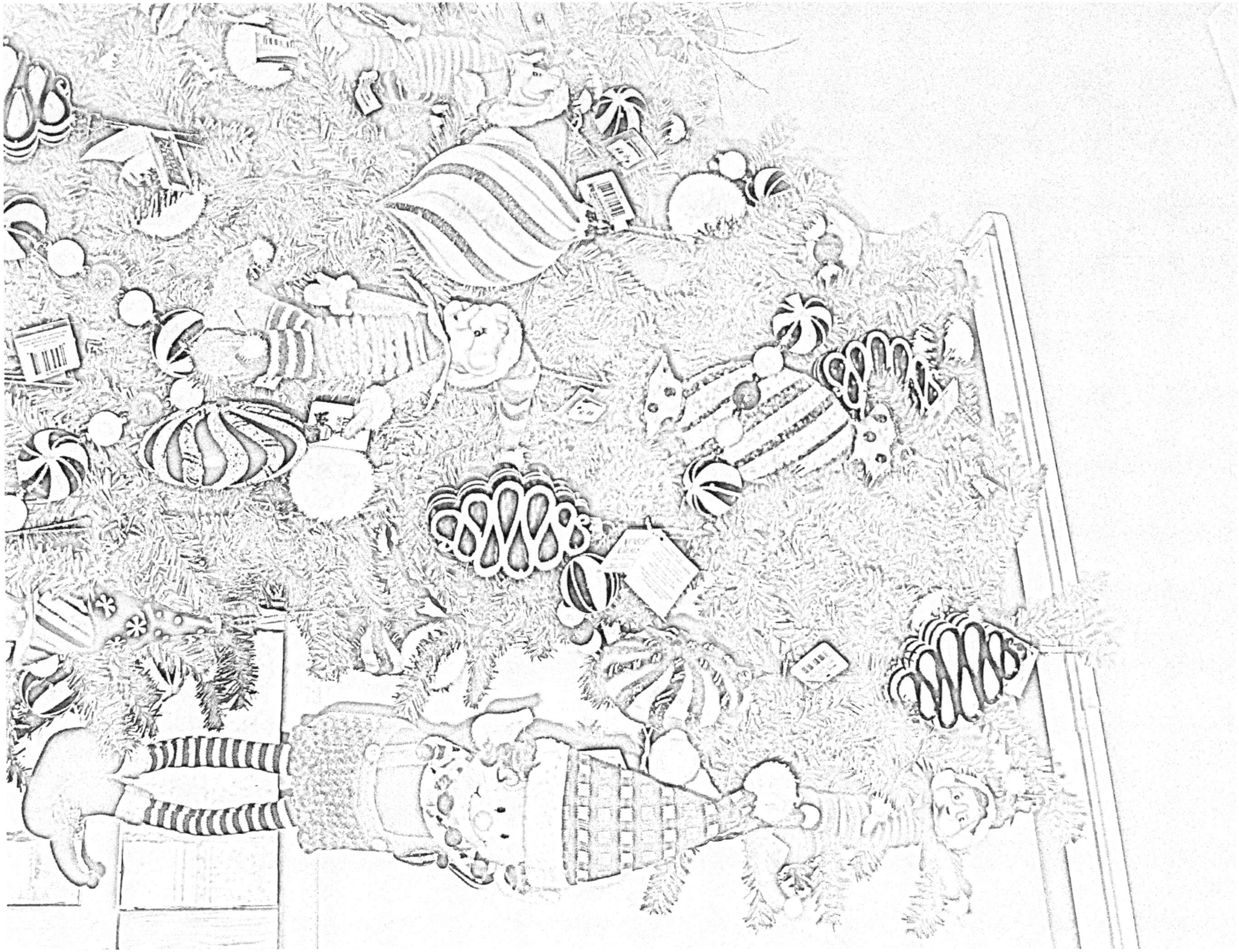

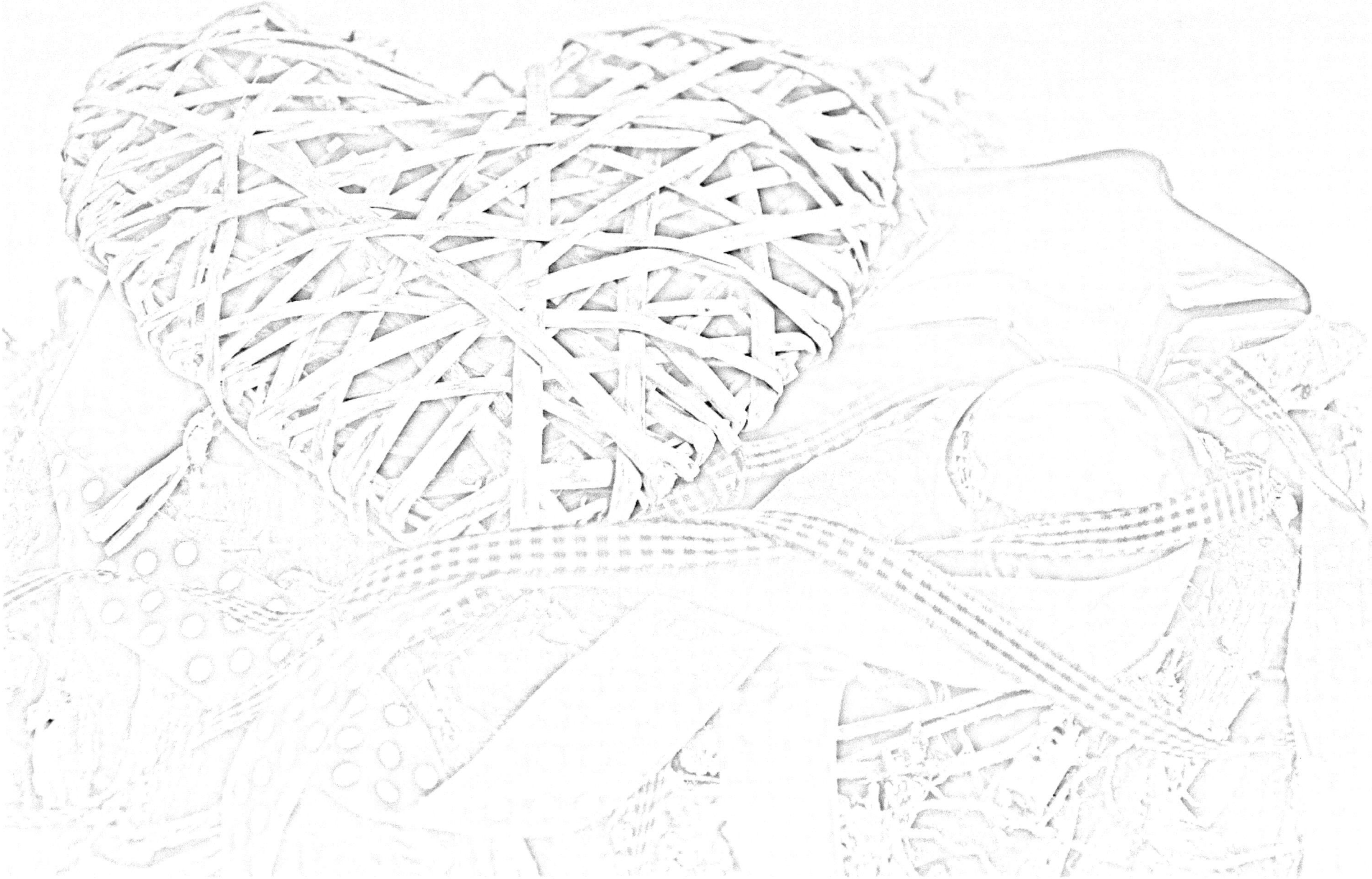

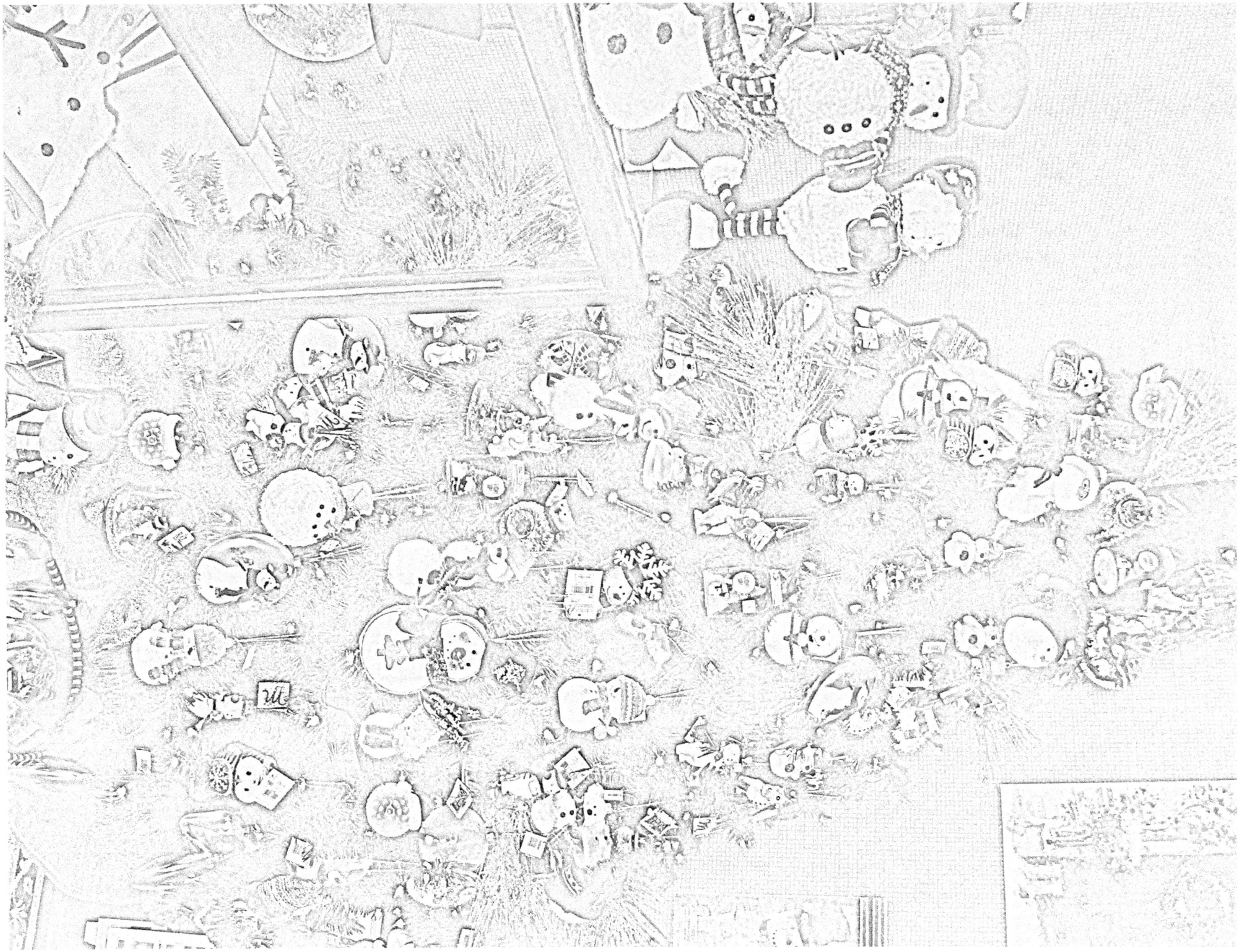

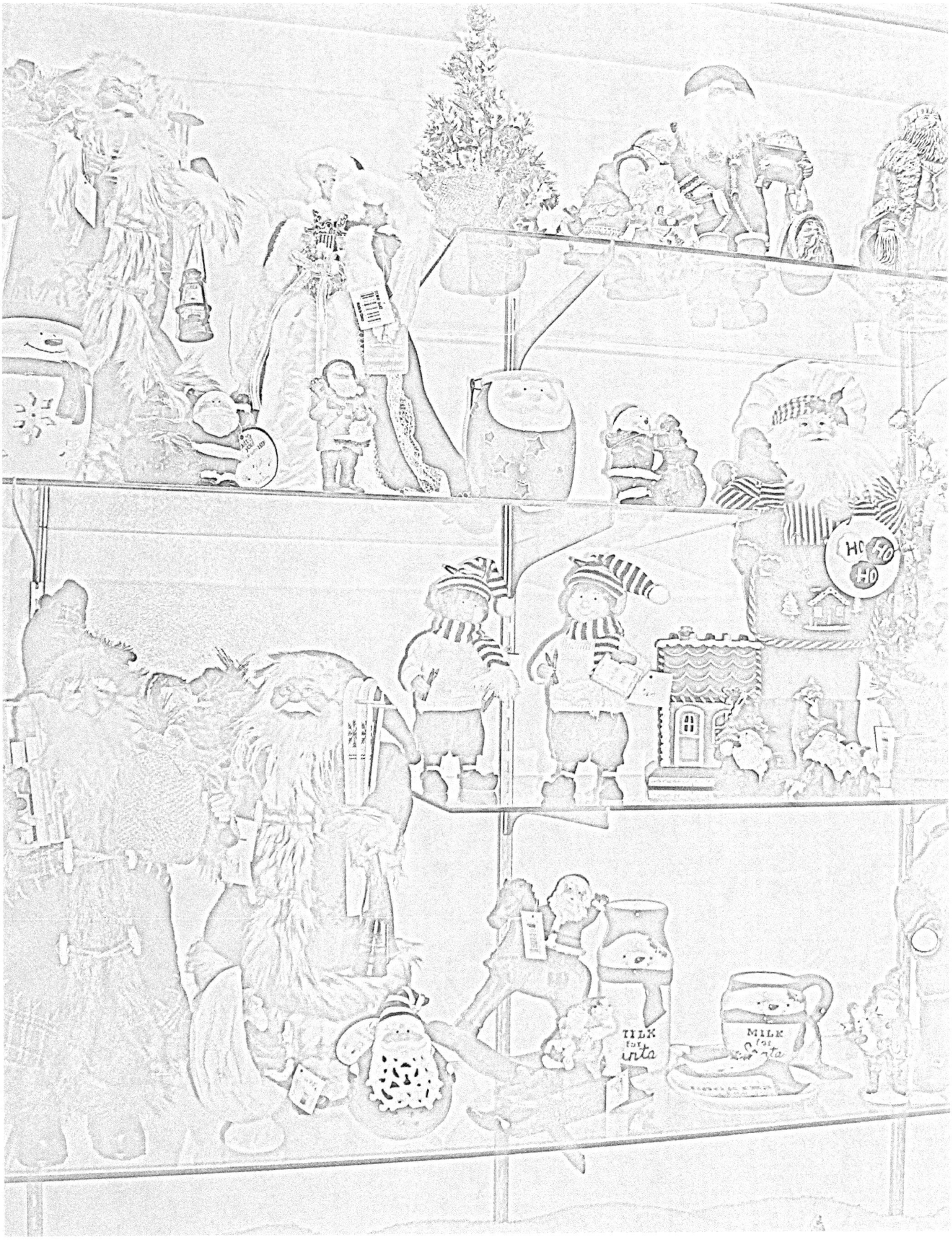
HO
HO
HO

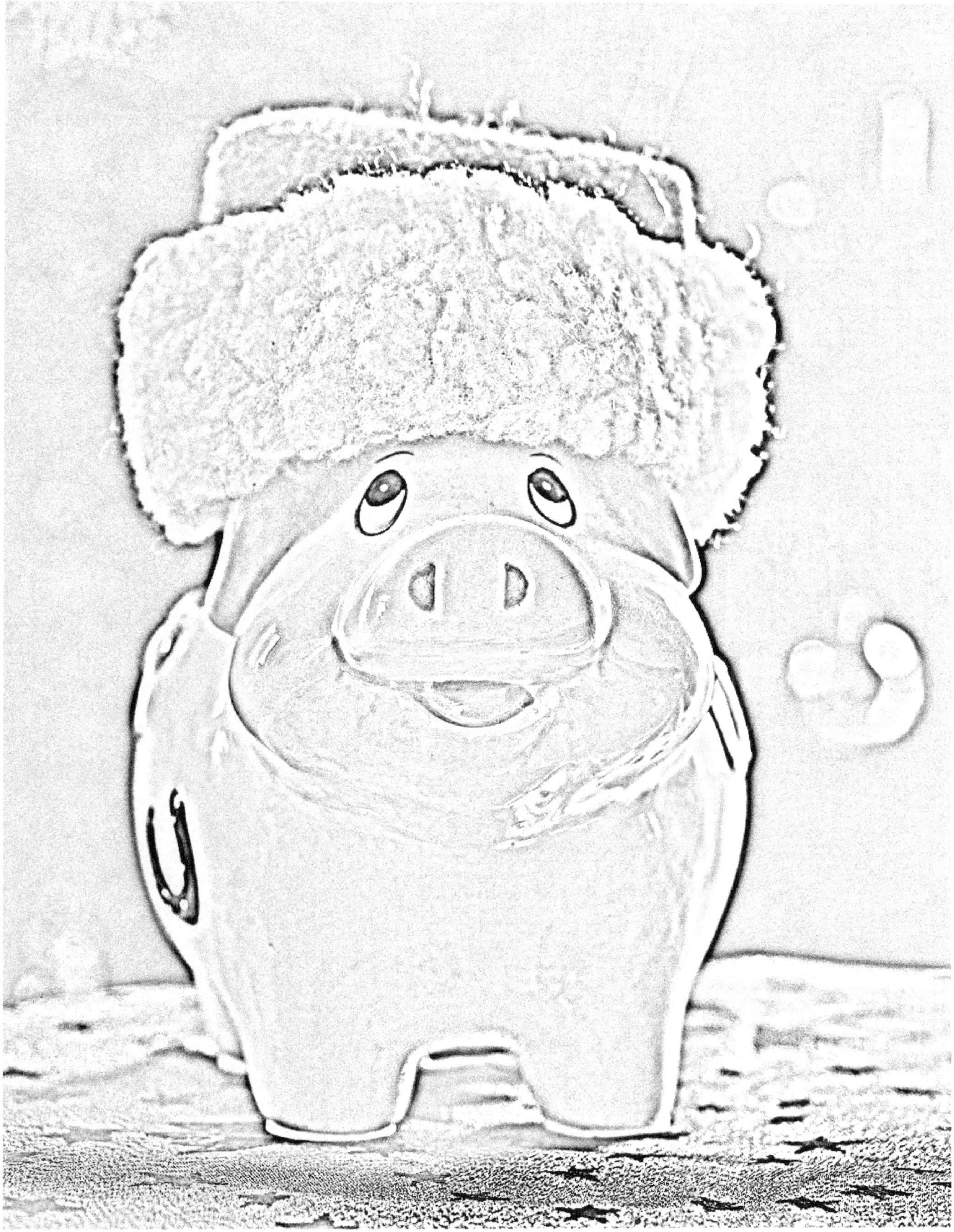

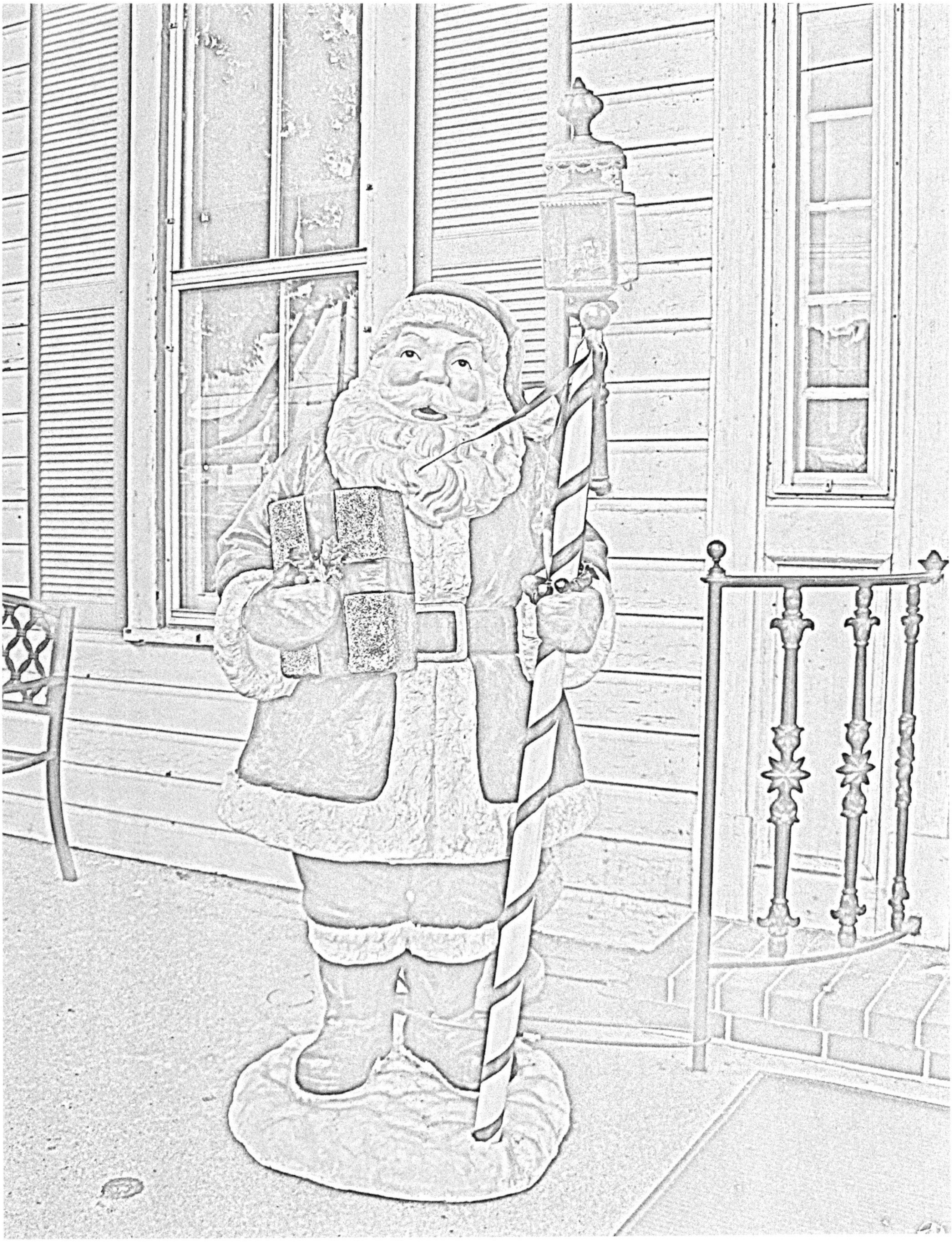

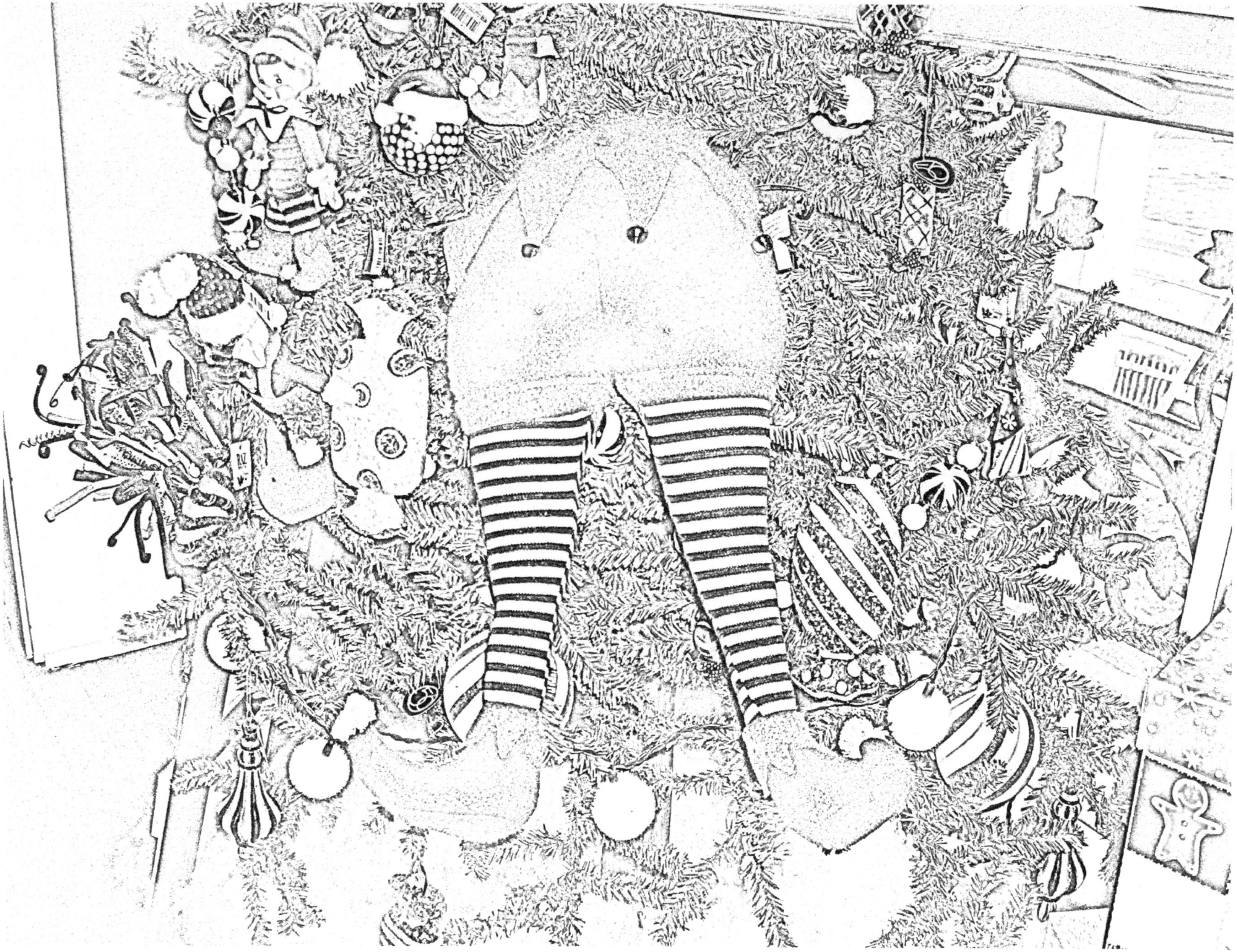

Merry Christmas!

We hope you enjoyed our book.

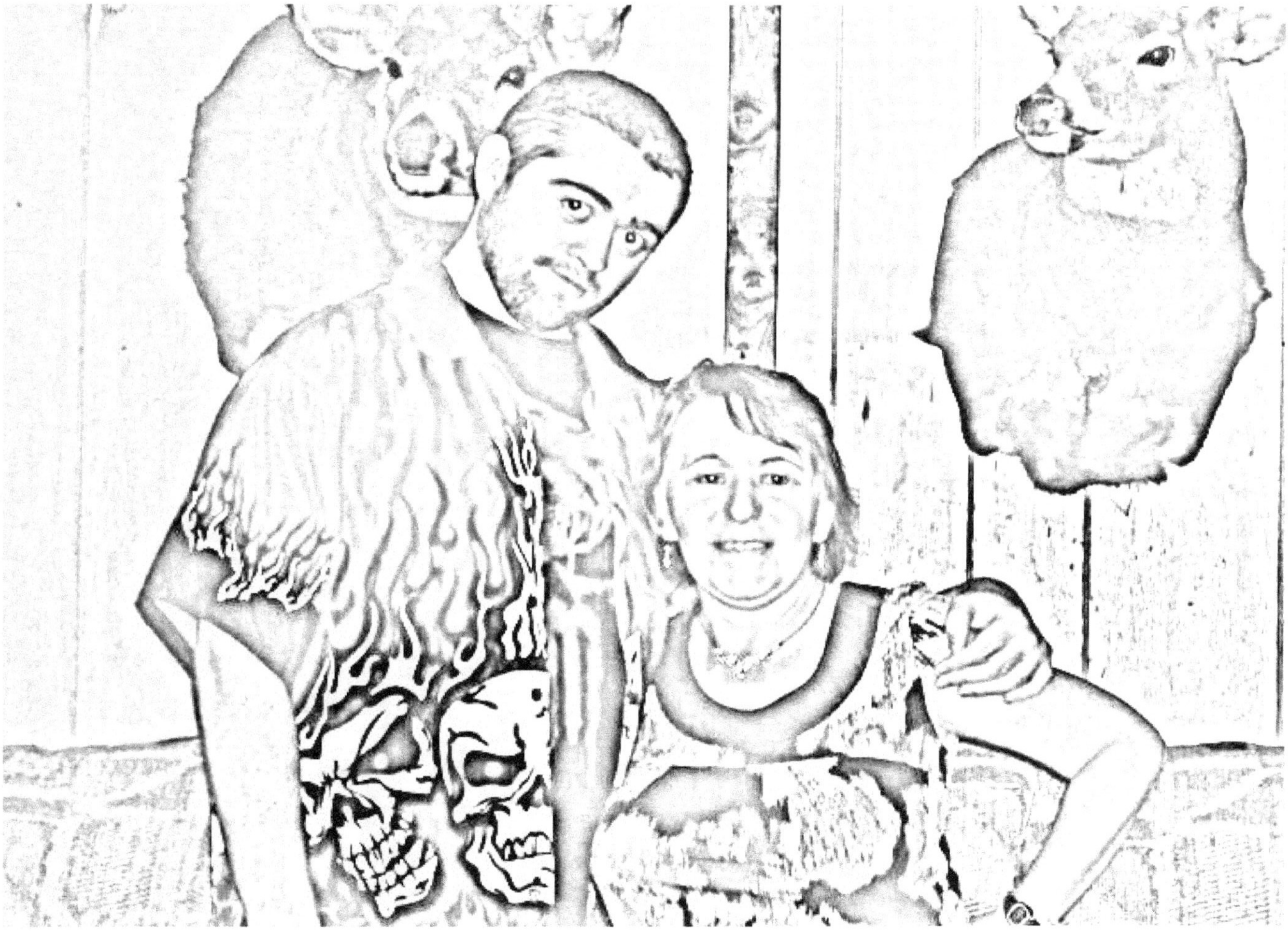

Watch for more coloring books by ARN Arts LLC.

http://arnarts.wixsite.com/books

www.ingramcontent.com/pod-product-compliance
Lightning Source LLC
Chambersburg PA
CBHW080630190526
45169CB00009B/3340
* 9 7 8 1 5 3 9 5 0 6 8 7 4 *